Ainsley Harriott's
Fresh and Fabulous
Meals in Minutes

Ainsley Harriott's Fresh and Fabulous Meals in Minutes

80 delicious time-saving recipes

Food photography by Francesca Yorke

BBC
BOOKS

10 9 8 7 6 5 4 3 2 1

Published in 2008 by BBC Books, an imprint of Ebury Publishing,
A Random House Group Company.
Originally published in hardback in 2007 as *The Feel-Good Cookbook*.

Copyright © Ainsley Harriott 2008

Author Name has asserted his/her right to be identified as the author of
this Work in accordance with the Copyright, Designs and Patents Act 1988

All photographs are by Francesca Yorke except those on pages 1, 136 and 150,
which are by Noel Murphy.

Photography © BBC Woodlands Ltd 2008

The Random House Group Limited Reg. No. 954009

Addresses for companies within the Random House Group can be found at
www.randomhouse.co.uk

A CIP catalogue record for this book is available from the British Library.

ISBN 978 1 846 07444 8

The Random House Group Limited makes every effort to ensure that the papers
used in our books are made from trees that have been legally sourced from well-
managed and credibly certified forests. Our paper procurement policy can be
found on www.randomhouse.co.uk

To buy books by your favourite authors and register for offers visit
www.rbooks.co.uk

Project editor: Eleanor Maxfield
Art Direction and Design: Smith & Gilmour, London
Home Economist: Annie Rigg

Printed and bound in Singapore by Tien Wah Press

Introduction

Welcome to Fresh and Fabulous Meals in Minutes ...

‘ I want you to enjoy these recipes –
bring them to life in your kitchen
and make cooking an enjoyable
and pleasurable art ... ,

Welcome to Fresh and Fabulous Meals in Minutes

Do you know, it's so interesting to discover things in life that actually make us feel good. Often it's the quite simple things such as learning to ride a bike, making your first butterfly cupcakes or scoring your first goal. Or maybe it's your first love, your first kiss, or getting your first pay cheque. But it's often difficult to find the time to do the simple things we enjoy, and we could all do with a bit more time to feel refreshed and good about ourselves.

When I started working on this book, I spent a lot of time asking people to summarise what feeling good meant to them. Their answers ranged from wearing their favourite jeans again after the birth of their child, to broader examples, such as the love of their family and spending time with friends. As I started to put the book together, I realised that so many of our memories involve experience – the more you try something, the better you become and the more rewarding it is.

It's almost the same in the kitchen: the more you do, the more experienced you become. And experimenting with wonderful produce and flavours becomes a way of life. I remember the first time I made the perfect soufflé. To be honest, I'd had a few mishaps along the way. However, I learnt a vital piece of information early on: a new broom sweeps clean, but an old broom knows the corners – now the soufflés rise perfectly every time! We shouldn't have to worry about the rules that can take the fun out of cooking. For example, I don't believe in being too strict with your diet and cutting out certain foods completely. There's no point having a big portion of something with no taste; better to have a small portion, including all the food groups, that really tastes of something. You shouldn't deny yourself an indulgent treat such as my **Chocolate heaven cake** (page 164) or refuse a good snack such as the steak in my **Gr8 steak and mushroom sandwiches** (page 84).

I've tried to structure the book so that you can find a fresh and fabulous fix for every occasion. This could be a much-needed brunch when you wake up after a big night out, or a simple snack when you've only got an hour to spare and don't want to resort to a supermarket ready-made meal. All of the meals can be cooked and prepared in sixty minutes or less. There are super-quick recipes when you've only got fifteen minutes to spare and healthy balanced meals in chapters such as *Quick and easy suppers* and *Substantial salads*. Of course, there are also chapters encouraging you to treat yourself with a wholesome snack or pudding. You'll find recipes that are good for your heart, good for boosting energy levels, good for your figure, good for having fun with, good for your soul, good for nights in and good for quick fixes. Anything that really gets you going and makes you feel fresh and fabulous again!

Cooking and your senses

We get so much out of our food! Each of our taste buds contain 50–100 receptor cells that send nerve impulses to our brain and really get us enthused. But to enjoy the full flavour of a Sunday roast or a chocolate mousse, you need the full sensory experience.

It's only when we pay attention to all of our senses that we get to know ingredients better and judge for ourselves what combinations of foods will provide a healthy balanced diet. Like every part of our body, our senses need a good workout – so get in there, get involved with the food and find out what you like.

Feels good . . .

Our bodies are telling us ways to feel good all the time. Liking sugar and salt, for example, satisfies our need for carbohydrates and minerals. Similarly, all you pregnant mums out there might be craving sour foods such as oranges and lemons that supply you with essential vitamins. Temperature and texture influence how much you appreciate foods. When you eat 'hot' foods like chilli peppers, you actually excite the pain receptors in your mouth.

Smells good . . .

Smell is important for getting nutrients from your food, which is not a function with which this sense is is commonly associated. Smelling your food prompts your body to produce digestive enzymes that are necessary for good digestion. The sense of smell also has a strong link to memory – how often has a delicious smell from the kitchen reminded you of a particular dish you enjoyed as a child?

Looks good . . .

These days we expect the food we enjoy in restaurants to look immaculate, but there is a lot to be said for the more 'rough and ready' look – where the juices and sauces are allowed to flow and all the layers of flavour are exposed to tempt us.

Sounds good, doesn't it?

Food has movement. It sizzles, crunches, oozes and splashes. It can be messy, but it triggers our appetite when we hear it. What could be a better wake-up call on a weekend morning than the sound of bacon sizzling in the pan?

But more important than anything else, I want you to enjoy these recipes – bring them to life in your kitchen and make cooking an enjoyable and pleasurable art rather than a frustrating and tedious pastime. Don't be intimidated; cooking can be so easy. We all know food is the fuel of life and with a little help from **Fresh and Fabulous Meals in Minutes** you can really enjoy it. So let's rattle those pots and pans and capture that fresh and fabulous moment!

How to use this book

It's amazing how much more aware of our food we are these days. You just need to walk around the supermarket and spot the people reading the backs of packets. Essentially, we all know what constitutes a healthy diet. For instance, I love to use a good olive oil when cooking – it's beneficial in lowering one's cholesterol levels and maintaining a healthy heart, and new research suggests it's an anti-inflammatory, too. I'm also very aware that we all need to reduce our daily salt intake – the average adult is eating 50% more salt than they should per day – 9.5 g instead of the recommended 6 g.

Having said that, you won't find any nutritional guidelines or analysis next to these recipes because cooking is all about listening to what your body is telling you and what your clothes are telling you! It's about applying a little common sense and getting the balance of your diet just right.

I've tried to make the chapters reflect our lifestyles, offering you new and exciting ways to spice up your meals throughout the day. In each chapter you'll find a few starting points to help you along with the fresh and fabulous philosophy – whether it's tips about creating a good atmosphere or where to source good ingredients.

Look out for the following:

▸ **Good for you boxes** These notes highlight aspects of the recipes that are particularly good for things such as your figure or your wallet

▸ ◕ **indicates recipes that can be cooked in fifteen minutes or less!**

▸ **'Fabulous feast'** spreads have ideas for grouping recipes together and creating a themed menu for entertaining guests. These can be found on pages 48, 129 and 151.

General guidelines for recipes

▸ All preparation and cooking times are approximate.

▸ The recipes supply metric and imperial measurements, but try not to mix and match.

▸ The recipes suggest using an all-purpose olive oil for cooking and extra-virgin olive oil for making salad dressings or marinades.

▸ As brands of salted butter vary, it is important to use unsalted butter where specified, especially for baking recipes.

▸ All teaspoon and tablespoon measurements are level unless stated otherwise.

▸ Recipes made with raw or lightly cooked eggs should be avoided by anyone who is pregnant or in a vulnerable health group.

Ainsley Harriott

Start the day the right way

Yoghurt with blueberry compote and crisp coconut honey oats

Serves 4–6
Preparation 10 mins
Cooking 10 mins
2 tablespoons clear honey
50 g (2 oz) porridge oats
50 g (2 oz) flaked almonds
25 g (1 oz) desiccated coconut
250 g (9 oz) blueberries
1 tablespoon caster sugar
juice of ½ lemon
1 x 500-g (17-fl oz) pot natural
    yoghurt

Good for your health
Blueberries are one of the most powerful foods – they're not only high in Vitamin C, but they also contain antioxidants which are said to reduce cholesterol.

For a great way to start off any brunch, this takes some beating. These crisp coconut honey oats keep well if stored in an airtight jar until needed, although I have to admit that they never last long in my house because they are rather moreish and make a good secret kitchen nibble! If you can't find blueberries, use other berries or soft dried apricots instead.

▸ Pour the honey into a frying pan. Add the oats, flaked almonds and coconut. Cook over a low heat for about 5 minutes, stirring constantly until golden (watch the pan carefully as the mixture can easily catch and burn if left unattended). Remove from the heat and tip on to a plate lined with baking parchment to get crisp.
▸ Put half the blueberries into a saucepan, add the sugar and lemon juice, and heat until the berries have burst and are really juicy. Add the remaining berries, remove from the heat and leave to cool.
▸ Divide the blueberries between glass tumblers or bowls. Cover with the yoghurt and scatter with the crisp oats. Serve immediately.

Fluffy smoked salmon omelette

This is a very indulgent brekkie – perfect for a special occasion.
Use organic eggs if possible and if you can't find salmon caviar (keta) replace it with any other kind. Double the quantities to make two omelettes.

▸ Beat the eggs together in a small bowl and season well. Cut the salmon into strips and fold into the beaten eggs.

▸ Heat the butter and oil in a 20-cm (8-inch) non-stick omelette pan and set over a medium heat. When the butter has melted and the foaming subsides, pour in the egg mixture. Allow the eggs to set for 10 seconds then, using a fork or spatula, quickly draw the edges of the omelette into the middle of the pan to allow the liquid egg to fill the space. When the eggs are almost set, tilt the pan away from you and, using a palette knife, fold one-third of the omelette into the centre and then fold over the other third.

▸ Slide the omelette on to a warm plate, cut a slit through the middle and spoon in the crème fraîche. Top with the salmon caviar, scatter with the chives and serve immediately.

Serves 1
Preparation 2 mins
Cooking 3 mins
3 medium eggs
1 slice smoked salmon
15 g (½ oz) butter
2 teaspoons sunflower oil
1 dessertspoon crème fraîche
1 dessertspoon salmon caviar
2 teaspoons snipped fresh chives
salt and freshly ground black pepper

Toasted muffins with crème fraîche, portabellini mushrooms and bacon bits

Serves 2
Preparation 5 mins
Cooking 10 mins

40 g (1 oz) butter
350 g (12 oz) portabellini or field
   mushrooms
1 teaspoon chopped fresh thyme
   leaves
1 small garlic clove, crushed
2 English muffins
3 rounded tablespoons crème fraîche
1 teaspoon Dijon mustard
50 g (2 oz) crispy bacon
salt and freshly ground black pepper

This makes a nice change from normal egg and bacon, and if you're vegetarian and leave out the bacon it's still really good. I use one of those convenient packets of cooked crispy bacon that supermarkets now sell. If you've got some chives or parsley handy, snip or chop them up and scatter over before serving.

▸ Melt the butter in a large frying pan over a medium heat. Thickly slice the mushrooms, add to the pan and cook for about 3 minutes, until starting to soften. Add the thyme and garlic and continue to cook for about 3 minutes, until the mushrooms are really tender and juicy.
▸ Meanwhile, split and toast the muffins.
▸ Add the crème fraîche, mustard and plenty of seasoning to the mushrooms. Allow the crème fraîche to melt, mix to combine, and bubble for about 30 seconds. Crumble or roughly chop the bacon and add to the pan. Arrange the muffins on warm plates, top with the creamy mushrooms and serve immediately.

Cocotte eggs with garlic and chorizo piperade

This recipe came about because I had some chorizo piperade left over from a few nights before, which I had served with grilled fish. However, it's just as nice as a breakfast dish. You could also try it as a side dish to grilled chicken.

▸ Heat the oil in a sauté pan over a medium heat, add the onion, pepper and garlic and cook for about 5 minutes, until starting to soften. Add the chorizo and continue to cook for a further 5 minutes, stirring from time to time. Add the tomatoes, sugar and some seasoning. Cover and cook over a low heat for 15 minutes, until the sauce has thickened and the vegetables are nice and soft. Divide the piperade between 6 x 150-ml (5-fl oz) ramekins and cool slightly.
▸ Preheat the oven to 180°C/350°F/Gas mark 4.
▸ Break an egg into each ramekin on top of the piperade. Season the cream, add cayenne or paprika and divide between the ramekins, pouring 2 tablespoons carefully over each egg.
▸ Set the ramekins in a small roasting tin and pour in enough boiling water to come halfway up their sides of the dishes. Carefully slide the roasting tin on to the middle shelf of the oven and bake for 12–15 minutes, until the eggs are almost set. Remove the ramekins from the roasting tin and serve immediately with hot buttered toast soldiers.

Serves 6
Preparation 25 mins
Cooking 20 mins
2 tablespoons olive oil
1 small onion, sliced
1 red pepper, seeded and sliced
1 garlic clove, crushed
75 g (3 oz) chorizo, skinned and diced
1 x 227-g (8-oz) can chopped
    tomatoes
pinch of caster sugar
6 large eggs
175 ml (6 fl oz) double cream
pinch of cayenne or paprika
salt and freshly ground black pepper

Quick tip
It's amazing what you can do with leftovers. Keep ingredients such as chorizo that can be used for dinner one night and breakfast the next.

Healthy breakfast bars to go

Makes about 20
Preparation 20 mins
Cooking 35 mins
175 g (6 oz) unsalted butter
100 g (4 oz) soft light brown sugar
4 tablespoons clear honey
350 g (12 oz) porridge oats
50 g (2 oz) sultanas
50 g (2 oz) flaked almonds
½ teaspoon ground cinnamon
1 tablespoon sesame seeds
  (optional)
1 tablespoon sunflower seeds
  (optional)
1 tablespoon pumpkin seeds
  (optional)
75 g (3 oz) ready-to-eat dried apricots
75 g (3 oz) stoned dates
50 g (2 oz) blanched hazelnuts
2 medium-sized ripe bananas

When time is against you, it's not always easy to start the day the proper way with a good healthy breakfast, but now you can with my nutritious grab-and-go breakfast bars. You could use maple syrup or golden syrup in place of honey, and any combination of nuts, dried fruit and seeds. Dried pineapple, mango or banana chips are all good, as are pecans, raisins and coconut. Use whole oats rather than the dusty flaky variety.

▸ Preheat the oven to 190°C/375°F/Gas mark 5. Grease a 23 x 30 x 5-cm (9 x 12 x 2-inch) baking tin with butter and line with baking parchment.
▸ In a saucepan combine the butter, sugar and honey and heat gently until melted, stirring from time to time. Simmer gently for 30 seconds, then remove from the heat.
▸ Place the oats in a large bowl, add the sultanas, almonds, cinnamon and seeds (if using). Chop the apricots and dates into 1-cm (½-inch) pieces and roughly chop the hazelnuts. Add to the bowl and mix well.
▸ Mash the bananas and mix into the butter and honey mixture. Pour into the oats and mix well until thoroughly combined. Tip into the prepared baking tin and press down in an even layer with a palette knife. Bake on the middle shelf of the oven for 30–35 minutes until golden.
▸ Cool in the tin, then cut into bars.

Quick tip
These bars are ideal for children's lunch boxes and they store well in an airtight container.

Crispy corned beef and beet hash

Beef hash is a great breakfast or brunch treat that's outstanding for tastiness and economy, and is popular in the US. With the addition of beetroot, this crunchy version goes a wicked purple-red colour. You could leave the beet out, but don't knock it till you've tried it.

▸ Peel the potatoes and cut into large dice. Cook in boiling salted water for about 10 minutes, or until just tender, then drain.

▸ Meanwhile, heat the oil in a large frying pan, add the onions and fry over a medium heat until beginning to brown at the edges.

▸ Add the drained potatoes and cook for 2 minutes before adding the corned beef and beetroot. Mix well, then cook for 3–4 minutes without turning to allow the bottom to crisp up.

▸ Continue to cook for a further 10 minutes, stirring as little as possible so that the potatoes, beetroot and corned beef cook down, and the mixture has plenty of crispy bits throughout.

▸ Season, scatter with the parsley and serve with sunnyside-up fried eggs.

Serves 4
Preparation 10 mins
Cooking 25 mins
500 g (1 lb 2 oz) floury potatoes
3 tablespoons olive oil
2 medium onions, sliced
1 x 340-g (12-oz) can corned beef, diced
150 g (5 oz) cooked beetroot, diced
1 tablespoon chopped fresh parsley
salt and freshly ground black pepper

Good for mums-to-be
Beetroot, with its deep red colour, is not surprisingly associated with love and was apparently popular with Aphrodite, the Greek goddess of love. It's high in folic acid, which helps the manufacture of red blood cells and is important for the first months of pregnancy.

Apple maple pancakes
with blackberry compote

Makes 18–20
Preparation 20 mins
Cooking 20 mins
2 red-skinned apples
1 tablespoon maple syrup
½ teaspoon ground cinnamon
2 teaspoons butter
150 g (5 oz) plain flour
½ teaspoon baking powder
pinch of salt
50 g (2 oz) caster sugar
175 ml (6 fl oz) milk
2 large eggs, separated
maple syrup, to serve

Blackberry compote
300 g (11 oz) blackberries or
   blueberries
1 tablespoon caster sugar

**It's such a shame that for many of us the only time we turn our hands
to** pancakes is on Shrove Tuesday because they are among the simplest
and most satisfying things to make. I bet you've been tempted by high
street crêperies, offering a range of buckwheat pancakes, or enjoyed
Russian blinis served with caviar and soured cream, or bao bing, the
thin Chinese pancakes we love to eat with shredded duck. One of my
favourites when skiing in Austria is *kaiserschmarren* – rich shredded
pancakes served with plum compote. Whatever you fancy, there's a
pancake for you. For this pancake treat, you can use blueberries if
blackberries are unavailable.

▸ Make the compote first. Place the blackberries in a small pan. Add
the sugar and cook over a low heat until tender and juicy. Remove from
the heat.
▸ Core but do not peel the apples, and slice into rings no thicker than a
£1 coin. You will need at least 18–20 slices. Place in a bowl, add the maple
syrup and cinnamon and mix to coat.
▸ Melt half the butter in a large frying pan over a medium heat. Add half
the sliced apples and cook for 30–60 seconds, until starting to soften.
Remove from the pan and cook the remaining apple slices. Wash and
dry the frying pan.
▸ Sift the flour, baking powder and salt into a medium-sized bowl. Add
the sugar and mix to combine. In a jug whisk together the milk and the
egg yolks, pour this into the dry ingredients and mix to make a smooth
batter. In a clean bowl whisk the egg whites until they will just stand
in stiff peaks. Gently fold into the batter.
▸ Lightly grease the frying pan with a little of the remaining butter and
place over a medium heat. Arrange four apple slices in the pan, 4–5 cm
(1½–2 inches) apart and spoon 1 rounded tablespoon of batter over each
slice. Cook until small bubbles appear on the surface of the pancakes and
their undersides are golden brown. Flip the pancakes over with a palette
knife and cook for a further minute. Transfer to a plate and keep warm
while you cook the remaining pancakes in the same way. You may need
to wipe the pan clean with kitchen paper after each batch.
▸ Serve the warm pancakes with the blackberry compote spooned over
and a generous glug of maple syrup.

Parmesan eggs with roasted field mushrooms and cherry tomatoes

Scrambled eggs never go amiss at breakfast time. Large cultivated field mushrooms are big and meaty, turning these eggs into a hearty brunch, and the tomatoes add sweetness and a dash of colour.

▸ Preheat the oven to 200°C/400°F/Gas mark 6.
▸ Lay the mushrooms, gill-side uppermost on a large baking tray and place the tomatoes alongside. Drizzle with the oil, add seasoning and cook on the middle shelf of the oven for about 15–20 minutes, until tender and juicy.
▸ Once the mushrooms and tomatoes are cooked, prepare the scrambled eggs. Beat the eggs with half the cream and plenty of seasoning. Melt the butter in a saucepan, add the egg mixture and cook over a low heat, stirring constantly with a wooden spoon until the eggs have cooked into creamy curds. Add the remaining cream and half the Parmesan.
▸ To serve, place two mushrooms on each warm plate, top with the scrambled eggs and scatter with the remaining Parmesan and the chives. Add the roasted tomatoes and serve immediately with warm toast.

Quick tip
Use inventive 'trimmings' to transform a classic dish into something fresh and fabulous.

Serves 4
Preparation 5 mins
Cooking 25 mins
8 large flat mushrooms, stalks trimmed
250 g (9 oz) cherry tomatoes on the vine
2–3 tablespoons olive oil
8 large eggs
4 tablespoons double cream
40 g (1½ oz) butter
4 tablespoons freshly grated Parmesan
2 tablespoons snipped fresh chives
salt and freshly ground black pepper

Fresh and fabulous boosters

We all know how important it is for our children to eat a good breakfast, but it's just as important for adults! So many of us are intent on making our evening meal the most substantial, but most of us need our biggest energy boost in the morning to help us get through the day. The problem is, if you're like me, breakfast time can vary from 7 in the morning to 2 in the afternoon ... dont ask! Regardless of our lifestyle, we're all looking for something tasty, wholesome and fulfilling in our breakfasts. There are all sorts of food groups that can provide us with the essential nutrients to match our needs. So, here are some great tips to satisfy your breakie or brunchy passions.

Power breakfasts

Fresh fruit can boost the immune system and is full of all the vital nutrients to keep our mind and body stimulated. Kiwis, for example, contain twice the vitamin C of an orange, as much potassium as a banana and as much fibre as a bowl of bran flakes! With my recipes, you don't just have to rely on a glass of OJ. Look out for other powerful foods such as coconut, eggs, beans, multi-grains and tomatoes – all of which are a great start to a well-balanced day. Try **Healthy breakfast bars to go** (page 20).

Recovery breakfasts

After a big night out, and with a day's work ahead of you – we all need a helping hand towards feeling our best. Alcohol is a diuretic, meaning that it dehydrates you, so you need to replace those fluids. You're also likely to be tired, needing protein, potassium and iron. Stock up on cheese, eggs, mushrooms, bread, tomatoes, spinach and bananas. Try **Toasted muffins with crème fraîche, portabellini mushrooms and bacon bits** (page 18).

Comfort breakfasts

What could be better for a weekend treat than starting the day with a sweet sticky bun? You've got the rest of the day to count the calories – butter, syrup and pastry at breakfast are all feel-good treats that are sometimes worth enjoying without the worry. Try **Apple maple pancakes with blackberry compote** (page 24).

Spinach, Cheddar and Parmesan muffins with a cream cheese centre

Makes 12
Preparation time 10 mins
Cooking time 25 mins
500 g (1 lb 2 oz) plain flour
4 teaspoons baking powder
pinch of salt
3 eggs beaten
250 ml (8 fl oz) milk
50 ml (2 fl oz) olive oil, plus extra
    for greasing
100 g (4 oz) Cheddar, grated
75 g (3 oz) Parmesan, grated
150 g (5 oz) cooked spinach, finely
    chopped
1 teaspoon hot pepper sauce
    (optional)
200 g (7 oz) cream cheese
25 g (1 oz) sesame seeds

We tend to think of muffins as sweet accompaniments to coffee, but the savoury end of the spectrum can be equally exciting, as you'll discover when you tuck into these delightfully surprising cheesy muffins.

▸ Preheat the oven to 200°C/400°F/Gas mark 6. Line a muffin tray with paper cases or grease the holes with a little oil.
▸ Sift the flour, baking powder and salt into a large bowl. Make a well in the centre of the flour, pour in the eggs, milk and oil and stir until just combined: do not overmix. Lightly fold in the Cheddar, Parmesan, spinach and hot pepper sauce (if using).
▸ Half-fill the muffin holes or paper cases with the mixture, then pipe or spoon about a tablespoon of cream cheese on top of each and cover with the remaining mixture. Sprinkle the sesame seeds on the muffins and bake in the middle of the oven for 20–25 minutes, or until golden and cooked through. Remove the muffins from the tray while still warm and serve.

Rarebit mushrooms Florentine with roasted cherry tomatoes

Serves 4
Preparation 5 mins
Cooking 20 mins
8 large flat mushrooms, stalks
    trimmed
250 g (9 oz) cherry tomatoes
2 tablespoons olive oil
175 g (6 oz) young leaf spinach
15 g (½ oz) butter
½ tablespoon plain flour
120 ml (4 fl oz) semi-skimmed milk
175 g (6 oz) Cheddar, grated
2 tablespoons fresh white
    breadcrumbs
1 teaspoon English mustard powder
2 teaspoons Worcestershire sauce
1 large egg yolk
2 tablespoons freshly grated
    Parmesan
freshly ground black pepper

Good for everyone
Low fat, full fat, salt or no salt
– there are so many strong
ingredients in this classic
recipe that you can cook it
to fit anyone's dietary needs.

A great twist on an old classic. You really don't need to add salt as there's plenty in the cheese and Worcestershire sauce. I use semi-skimmed milk for this as the recipe is quite rich enough. For a lower-fat version use half milk and half cider to make the sauce. And remember, the leftover egg white can be kept in an ice tray in the freezer to use at a later date.

▸ Preheat the oven to 200°C/400°F/Gas mark 6.
▸ Lay the mushrooms, gill-side uppermost, on a baking tray, add the tomatoes and drizzle with the oil. Bake for about 10 minutes, until the mushrooms and tomatoes are slightly charred and starting to soften.
▸ Microwave or steam the spinach until wilted, then cool slightly and squeeze out any excess moisture.
▸ Preheat the grill. Melt the butter in a saucepan over a medium heat, add the flour and cook for 30 seconds, stirring constantly. Whisk in the milk, bring to the boil and cook for 1 minute until thickened. Remove from the heat, add the Cheddar, breadcrumbs, mustard and Worcestershire sauce. Mix well, beat in the egg yolk and season with pepper.
▸ Arrange the spinach on top of the mushrooms, spoon over the cheese sauce and scatter with the Parmesan. Slide the rarebit mushrooms and tomatoes under the grill and cook until the cheese is golden brown and bubbling. Serve immediately.

Light bites

Pea, mint and spinach soup

Serves 4–6
Preparation 5 mins
Cooking 25 mins
1 tablespoon olive oil
25 g (1 oz) butter
1 onion, chopped
1 leek, chopped
1 fat garlic clove, crushed
225 g (8 oz) floury potatoes, peeled
   and chopped
1. 2 litres (2 pints) vegetable stock
250 g (9 oz) frozen garden peas,
   defrosted
75 g (3 oz) young leaf spinach,
   washed
2 tablespoons chopped fresh mint
salt and freshly ground black pepper
crème fraîche, to serve

This beautiful bright green soup is a taste of spring, but it can be enjoyed at any time of the year. Use frozen peas rather than fresh ones as they give a much better texture. This recipe creates very little washing-up – just blend the soup base until smooth, add the peas and spinach and blend again.

▸ Heat the oil and butter in a large saucepan. Add the onion and leek and cook over a low heat for about 10 minutes, until tender but not coloured. Add the garlic and cook for a further 30 seconds.
▸ Add the potatoes to the pan. Pour in the stock and bring to the boil. Reduce the heat and simmer gently for about 15 minutes, until the potatoes are tender when tested with the point of a knife.
▸ Pour the soup into a blender and whiz until smooth. Add the peas and spinach and blend again until the soup is bright green and almost smooth. Pour back into the pan, add the mint, then season and reheat gently.
▸ Pour the soup into warm bowls, add a dollop of crème fraîche and a twist of pepper, and serve immediately.

Camembert and cranberry puff pastry pyramids

Serves 4
Preparation 10 mins
Cooking 20 mins
200 g (7 oz) puff pastry
plain flour, for rolling out
1 heaped tablespoon cranberry
   sauce, plus extra to serve
1 x 250-g (9-oz) whole Camembert
1 small egg
1 tablespoon milk

Choose a Camembert that is plump and yielding, and avoid any that are sunken and hard with a bitter smell.

Any sharp/sweet fruit condiment works well in this recipe. I also like to use quince or redcurrant jelly, which is often lurking around the fridge. Any leftover pastry can be sprinkled with grated cheese and made into cheese straws.

For a change, you can make this dish as four separate portions. Use 4–5 sheets of buttered filo pastry for each, and squeeze the corners of the layers together to create cheesy 'money bags'.

▸ Lightly dust a work surface with flour and roll the pastry out into a 23-cm (9-inch) square. Trim the edges.
▸ Spoon the cranberry sauce into the middle of the pastry and place the Camembert on top.
▸ Brush the edges of the square with a little water and bring the corners together to meet in the middle. Pinch the edges together to completely encase the cheese. Place on a parchment-lined baking sheet and refrigerate for 30 minutes.
▸ Preheat the oven to 220°C/425°F/Gas mark 7.
▸ Mix together the egg and milk and brush this over the pastry. Bake on the middle shelf of the oven for about 20 minutes, or until golden brown.
▸ Allow to rest for 2 minutes. To serve, cut into slices and accompany with lots of crusty French bread, extra cranberry sauce and a crisp green salad.

French toast, Italian cheese and British bacon sandwich

I could have called this the EU sandwich, but either way it tastes great.
I like to use ciabatta for this sandwich, but any nice bread will do. If the slices are large, you'll need extra eggs and milk. The gooey mozzarella makes it fun to eat. If you're in a hurry, buy a packet of crispy bacon rashers from a supermarket: most chains now sell them.

▸ Preheat the grill.
▸ Cook the bacon under the grill until crisp and golden.
▸ Lay out four slices of ciabatta. In a small bowl mix the tomatoes with the tomato paste and spread this on the bread. Cut the mozzarella into eight slices and place on top of the tomatoes, followed by the crispy bacon. Top with the remaining slices of bread.
▸ In a large bowl beat the eggs together with the cream or milk, season and pour into a flat dish. Dip each sandwich into the egg mixture, pushing down firmly so that it stays together.
▸ Heat the butter or butter and oil in a large frying pan over a low to medium heat until just beginning to foam. Add the sandwiches and cook for 1–2 minutes on each side, or until the egg is cooked and the sandwiches are golden brown. Cut them in half diagonally and serve immediately.

Serves 4–6
Preparation 10 mins
Cooking none
600 g (1 lb 6 oz) celeriac
juice of ½ lemon
4 rounded tablespoons mayonnaise
2 rounded teaspoons Dijon mustard
2 tablespoons crème fraîche
1 tablespoon chopped fresh parsley
2 teaspoons chopped fresh tarragon
   (optional)
150 g (5 oz) French beans
150 g (5 oz) cooked prawns
salt and freshly ground black pepper

Fresh and fabulous alfresco

There's no doubt about it, one of the most enjoyable ways of eating food is alfresco. There's something about being out in the fresh air that stimulates our appetite. Perhaps it's to do with the preparation: the making, the baking, the wrapping and the unwrapping. Ladies, gentleman and children – welcome to the picnic rap! I like mine with roast vegetables, hummus and goats' cheese (page 87), but my **Gr8 steak and mushroom sandwiches** are to die for (page 84). These days, eating outside is an elaborate affair. You can buy all sorts of gas cookers, foldable tables, neatly-packed utensils and gadgets from department or camping stores, so there's no excuse – eat out in style. Here are a few inspirational tips to make your alfresco event even better.

It's all in the basket
Invest in a good sturdy picnic basket so that the lovely food you've spent hours preparing can be enjoyed as it should be instead of squashed at the bottom of plastic carrier bags. You could even get a pre-packed one.

Barbecue simple
It's too difficult to keep, store and shift lots of different ingredients, so try cooking one whole fish either on a fish rack or wrapped in foil, or a whole boned-out marinated leg of lamb. Don't forget good-quality sausages and burgers for the kids!

The thermos is back
Not just for the ramblers and truck drivers, portable drinks have come a long way. So you can have your hot soup in the Cotswold countryside after all. Don't forget you can chill drinks in a thermos, too.

Don't compromise on style
I don't know about you, but I hate paper plates. Having said that, you can get some great plastic ones in lovely bright colours. You can even get plastic wine goblets so you don't have to worry about all that glass as the kids are running around. Bring along basil and mint to garnish all your lovingly prepared food. And it's always nice to have real napkins.

It's your picnic so enjoy it!

Celeriac remoulade with prawns and French beans

Serves 4
Preparation 10 mins
Cooking 5 mins
8 rashers rindless streaky bacon
8 slices ciabatta bread
8–10 sun-blushed tomatoes, chopped
4 tablespoons sun-dried tomato paste
1 x 200-g (7-oz) packet mozzarella
4 medium free-range eggs
4 tablespoons cream or full-fat milk
50 g (2 oz) butter, or half butter and half olive oil
salt and freshly ground black pepper

A remoulade without celeriac is like strawberries without cream. The dish has long been one of the great delights of French cuisine, and once tried, it often becomes a favourite. Make sure you use the best-quality mayonnaise.

This recipe is delicious on its own with some good, crusty bread, but you can throw in some cooked mussels in season and also add peas and broad beans. If your French beans are nice and fresh, simply top them and leave the tails on because they look really pretty in the salad.

▸ Peel the celeriac, cut it into big chunks and coarsely grate or shred the chunks. This is easily done with the shredding blade in a food processor. Toss in the lemon juice to prevent discolouring.
▸ In a large bowl mix together the mayonnaise, mustard and crème fraîche. Season well and add the herbs. Add the celeriac and mix until thoroughly combined.
▸ Fill a pan with water, add some salt and bring to the boil. Meanwhile, top and tail the French beans and cut into 2.5-cm (1-inch) lengths. Cook in the boiling water for 2–3 minutes, until tender. Drain in a colander, then refresh under cold running water and pat dry with kitchen paper. Add the beans and prawns to the celeriac and gently mix to combine. Chill, or serve immediately with lots of crunchy French bread.

Curried sweet potato soup with chicken and spinach

Another easy dish for using up any leftover roast chicken pieces.
Sweet potatoes are a great alternative to normal potatoes and they add a vibrant colour to this soup.

▸ Heat the butter and oil in a large saucepan. Add the onion, leek and celery to the pan and cook over a low to medium heat for about 5 minutes, until tender but not coloured. Add the garlic, chilli and curry powder and continue to cook for a further minute.

▸ Peel the sweet potatoes and cut into chunks. Add to the pan with the stock, season and bring to the boil. Lower the heat, half-cover the pan and simmer for about 20–25 minutes, until the potatoes are tender.

▸ Purée the soup until smooth using either a blender or hand-held mixer. Add a little extra stock if the mixture is too thick, and check the seasoning.

▸ Add the chicken to the pan with the spinach. Simmer for a further minute until the chicken has heated through and the spinach has wilted. Ladle into warm bowls and sprinkle a little nutmeg over each bowl. Serve with warm garlic naan breads.

Quick tip
If you don't have leftovers, buy prepared roast meat pieces from the supermarket.

Serves 4–6
Preparation 10 mins
Cooking 40 mins
25 g (1 oz) butter
1 tablespoon olive oil
1 onion, chopped
1 leek, chopped
1 stick celery, chopped
2 garlic cloves, crushed
pinch of crushed dried chilli
2 teaspoons mild curry powder
3 medium-sized sweet potatoes
1.2 litres (2 pints) chicken or
   vegetable stock
3 cooked chicken breasts, shredded
75 g (3 oz) young leaf spinach
freshly grated nutmeg
salt and freshly ground black pepper

Prawn and coconut laksa

Serves 4
Preparation 10 mins
Cooking 20 mins

1 x 400-ml (14-fl oz) can coconut milk
2 tablespoons sunflower oil
400 ml (14 fl oz) light chicken
　or fish stock
1 tablespoon fish sauce
1 tablespoon soft light brown sugar
250 g (9 oz) fine egg noodles
24 raw tiger prawns, shelled and
　deveined
100 g (4 oz) bean sprouts, rinsed
4 spring onions, chopped
2 tablespoons roughly chopped
　fresh coriander
lime wedges, to serve

Curry paste
1 red chilli, seeded and chopped
1 stick lemon grass, roughly chopped
1 tablespoon freshly grated ginger
1 teaspoon ground turmeric
1 teaspoon ground coriander
2 garlic cloves, crushed
2 shallots or ½ onion, roughly
　chopped

I've been lucky enough to visit Thailand many times, and good food is essential to the convivial pleasures of life there; they refer to this as *sanuk*, which means 'enjoyable and good fun', or *sabal*, meaning 'deliciously satisfied'. Thais certainly understand how to blend flavours – they make their dishes fiery with chillies and scent them with ingredients such as basil, coriander, lemon grass, garlic, shallots, ginger, tamarind and kaffir lime.

Imagine a gorgeous coconut broth (laksa) laced with a fragrant Thai curry paste, fresh prawns, noodles and crunchy bean sprouts. I often make this at home, and it takes only 20 minutes to cook. The coconut broth is a base to which all sorts of foods can be added: try it with fresh fish, cooked chicken, rice noodles, bamboo shoots or pak choi leaves.

▸ Make the curry paste first. Place all the paste ingredients in the bowl of a food processor or blender. Add 75 ml (3 fl oz) of the coconut milk and whiz to a paste, scraping down the sides with a rubber spatula.
▸ Heat the oil in a large pan, add the curry paste and cook for 2 minutes over a lowish heat to allow all the flavours to release their delicious aromas. Add the remaining coconut milk, stock, fish sauce and brown sugar. Bring to the boil, reduce to a simmer and cook for 10–15 minutes.
▸ Meanwhile, cook the noodles in boiling water according to the packet instructions.
▸ Add the prawns to the broth and simmer until they change colour and are cooked through. Add the bean sprouts and cook for a further 30 seconds.
▸ Divide the noodles between four warm bowls and ladle the soup, prawns and bean sprouts on top. Scatter with the spring onions and coriander, and serve immediately with lime wedges to squeeze over.

Quick tip
This curry paste can be made in advance and kept in the fridge or freezer.

Carrot and parsnip soup with garlic and thyme croutons

This smooth, creamy orange soup is absolutely perfect for a dinner party as you can make it in advance – and is equally delicious as a light bite.

Organic carrots are best and only need to be scrubbed before use. Croutons are best made with day-old bread, and if it's sourdough, so much the better.

▸ Heat the oil and butter in a large pan over a low to medium heat. Add the onion, celery and carrots to the pan and cook for about 10 minutes, until tender but not coloured. Add the garlic and cook for a further minute.

▸ Add the parsnips to the pan with the stock and sugar. Season well and bring to the boil, then half-cover the pan and reduce the heat to a gentle simmer. Cook for about 30 minutes, until the vegetables are tender.

▸ Pour the soup into a blender and whiz until smooth, or blend directly in the pan using a hand-held blender. Pour the soup back into the pan, check the seasoning and heat gently while you make the croutons.

▸ Cut the slices of bread into cubes. Place the olive oil in a large frying pan, add the garlic and heat slowly over a low flame so that the garlic infuses the oil. Increase the heat under the pan and add the bread cubes and thyme. Cook until the croutons are golden and crisp, stirring constantly. Remove from the pan with a slotted spoon, drain on kitchen paper and season well.

▸ Ladle the soup into warm bowls, drizzle crème fraîche over the top and scatter with the garlicky croutons.

Serves 4–6
Preparation 10 mins
Cooking 45 mins
1 tablespoon olive oil
25 g (1 oz) butter
1 onion
1 stick celery, chopped
350 g (12 oz) carrots, chopped
1 garlic clove, crushed
2 medium parsnips, peeled, chopped
1.2 litres (2 pints) vegetable stock
pinch of sugar
salt and freshly ground black pepper
crème fraîche, to serve

Garlic and thyme croutons
4 slices bread
4–5 tablespoons olive oil
2 large garlic cloves, sliced
3 teaspoons chopped fresh thyme
  leaves

Good for your eyes
The darker the carrot, the more beta-carotene it contains, which is essential for healthy eyes.

Grilled asparagus with smoked salmon, poached eggs and chive hollandaise

Serves 2
Preparation 5 mins
Cooking 10 mins
250 g (9 oz) bunch English
   asparagus, trimmed
1 tablespoon olive oil
2 English muffins
2 large eggs
4 slices (125 g/4 oz) smoked salmon
2 teaspoons **Hollandaise sauce**
   (page 178)
1 tablespoon snipped fresh chives
salt and freshly ground black pepper

I love the fresh bundles of asparagus you can buy at farmers' markets. The English asparagus season starts in May and this is a perfect – and indulgent – way to enjoy it!

▶ Preheat a ridged griddle pan. Fill a sauté pan with salted water and bring to a simmer.
▶ Toss the asparagus in the oil and season. Grill on the griddle pan for about 4 minutes until tender – you will need to keep turning the asparagus to prevent it burning. Split the muffins and toast the cut sides on the griddle pan or under the grill.
▶ Meanwhile, break each egg into a teacup or small bowl. Using a spoon, swirl the simmering water in the sauté pan and drop one egg at a time into the water. Cook for 2–3 minutes depending on how well done you like the yolks. Remove from the water with a slotted spoon and drain quickly on kitchen paper.
▶ Place the toasted muffins on warm plates and arrange the chargrilled asparagus on top. Drape two slices of smoked salmon over each portion and spoon the hollandaise sauce over the salmon. Place the poached eggs on top. Scatter with the chives and serve immediately.

Fabulous feast: The Middle East

I particularly like the recipes in this *Light bites* chapter because you get a full range of beautiful flavours – and you can mix and match lighter dishes to put together a bigger meal if you need to.

Food from the Middle East combines lots of recipes that are considerably different in culture and flavour so you're sure to get a full range of great-tasting salads and starters, fresh spices and herbs and all sorts of breads and wonderful dips. It's a great theme for those occasions when you get together with friends for a good natter and want a few small dishes that you can dip into and share.

You can use the recipes in this book to put on your own exotic Middle Eastern spread. Most of the dishes store well in the fridge so can be reheated at a moment's notice. Your guests can eat as little or as much as they like and the conversation starts rolling as everyone compares the delicious food on offer.

Start with plenty of light appetisers or *mezzeh*. These are often eaten with pitta bread or you could try the traditional *lavash* – a type of cracker bread that is available from Greek or Turkish markets. Other ingredients you could experiment with include delicious honey, sesame seeds, sumac, chickpeas, mint and parsley.

Menu ideas

A selection of *mezzeh* to share
Pea, mint and spinach soup **page 34**
Roasted vegetable wraps with hummus and goats' cheese **page 87**
Flash-fried goats' cheese with grape and chilli chutney **page 56**
Brown basmati and mottled bean salad **page 76**
The other Greek salad **page 81**

To follow
Lamb meatballs in tomato sauce with couscous **page 130**
Roasted Ramiro peppers stuffed with goats' cheese and garlic crumbs **page 175**

Dessert
Prunes and figs infused in tea with vanilla bean yoghurt **page 168**
Lemon surprise pudding with ginger-spiced cream **page 154**

Pan-seared Mumbai mackerel with Waldorf salad

The perfect partner for these spiced mackerel fillets is a crisp, classic salad lightly dressed in crème fraîche and mayonnaise. Use a good-quality curry powder and make sure it's not out of date (it happens to the best of us). Get the fishmonger to fillet and bone the mackerel for you.

▸ Prepare the Waldorf salad first. Shred the cabbage as finely as possible or use the large grating disc/blade on your food processor. Place in a large bowl with the apples, celery, onions and walnuts and toss together. Add the crème fraîche and mayonnaise, season and mix well to coat everything nicely.
▸ Season each mackerel fillet with a good dusting of curry powder, salt and pepper.
▸ Heat the olive oil in a large frying pan over a medium-high heat. Add a knob of butter (about a teaspoonful) followed immediately by the spiced mackerel fillets. Cook skin-side down for about 1 minute, until the skin is crisp. Flip the fillets over and cook the other sides for about 30–60 seconds, until cooked through. You may need to cook the fish in batches, in which case keep the first lot warm while you fry the remainder.
▸ Divide the Waldorf salad between four plates and serve the mackerel fillets criss-crossed on top with lemon wedges to squeeze over.

Serves 4
Preparation 10 mins
Cooking 5 mins
4 medium mackerel, filleted
    and boned
2 tablespoons mild curry powder
2 tablespoons olive oil
few knobs of butter
salt and freshly ground black pepper
lemon wedges, to serve

Waldorf salad
¼ head white cabbage
2 small apples, such as Cox's orange
    pippins, cored and diced
2 sticks celery, sliced
3 spring onions, sliced
50 g (2 oz) toasted walnuts,
    roughly chopped
1 heaped tablespoon crème fraîche
1 heaped tablespoon mayonnaise

**Good for getting
the balance right**
Here's a dish that can be worked into a perfectly healthy, balanced diet. It covers many essential food groups: a recommended serving of oily fish, low-fat crème fraîche and plenty of veggies in one hit.

Parmesan, goats' cheese and Stilton nugget soufflés

Serves 6
Preparation 30 mins
Cooking 10–15 mins
65 g (2½ oz) butter
4 tablespoons finely grated
    Parmesan
40 g (1½ oz) plain flour
250 ml (9 fl oz) milk
100 g (4 oz) crumbly goats' cheese
pinch of cayenne
4 medium eggs, separated
1 medium egg white
100 g (4 oz) Stilton
salt and freshly ground black pepper

Soufflés are not difficult to make and don't demand lots of kitchen skills – as my 12-year-old daughter Maddie proved to her school chums when I wasn't even around to give her a helping hand. The ones she made were lovely and golden, with a light, moist texture, and the Cheddar flavour came bursting through. She remembered three important points:

1. The base, a white sauce or pastry cream for sweet soufflés.
2. A flavouring i.e. cheese, chocolate.
3. Beaten egg whites for a light texture and the perfect rise.
You can also take heart from the knowledge that it's quite often the freshness of the eggs, not you, that determines whether a soufflé succeeds or not, so don't beat yourself up if it doesn't work out.

▸ Preheat the oven to 200°C/400°F/Gas mark 6.
▸ Melt 25 g (1 oz) of the butter and brush half of it over the insides of 6 x 150-ml (5-fl oz) ramekins. Dust over this coating with 1 tablespoon of the Parmesan. Chill the ramekins for 10–15 minutes. Brush with the remaining melted butter, scatter with another tablespoon of Parmesan, then chill until needed.
▸ Melt the remaining butter in a small pan, add the flour and cook for 30 seconds. Gradually add the milk and bring to the boil, stirring constantly until smooth and thickened. Simmer for 30 seconds to cook the flour. Remove from the heat and pour into a large bowl. Cool slightly, then stir in the goats' cheese and remaining Parmesan. Add the cayenne and some seasoning.
▸ Beat the egg yolks into the cheese mixture until they are thoroughly incorporated.
▸ In another large, clean bowl whisk the five egg whites until they hold stiff peaks. Add a large spoonful of the beaten egg whites to the cheese sauce and stir it in to loosen the mixture. Using a large metal spoon, fold the remaining egg whites into the sauce.
▸ Divide the soufflé mixture between the ramekins – they should be no more than three-quarters full – and place on a baking sheet. Cook on the middle shelf of the oven for about 10–15 minutes, until golden brown and well risen. Quickly transfer to warm plates, and push a nugget of Stilton into the centre of each soufflé. Serve immediately.

Bruschetta with tomatoes, roasted peppers and marinated anchovies

It's always nice to have a few pre-dinner nibbles at hand, and if you want to be more adventurous than the nuts and multiflavoured crisps brigade, these delicious and colourful bruschetta never fail to impress.

You could roast red peppers for this recipe, but it's quicker and easier to use the ready-prepared ones in jars. Look out for the wood-roasted variety, which tastes divine. If you're not a lover of anchovies, just leave them out, but they do add a little something extra.

▸ Core the tomatoes and roughly chop the flesh. Dice the peppers and roughly chop the olives. Mix together and season well.
▸ Toast the slices of bread under the grill or on a ridged griddle pan. Spread with the pesto and top with the tomato mixture. Slice the anchovies, arrange on top and serve immediately.

Serves 6
Preparation 10 mins
Cooking 2 mins
4 large, ripe tomatoes
50–75 g (2–3 oz) roasted red peppers
1 rounded tablespoon pitted black olives
6 slices sourdough bread
4–6 tablespoons **Home-made pesto** (page 185)
6 marinated anchovies
salt and freshly ground black pepper

Bloody Mary prawn and avocado cocktail

Serves 4–6
Preparation 10 mins +
20 mins marinating
Cooking none
3 ripe tomatoes, seeded and chopped
4 spring onions, finely sliced
1 red chilli, seeded and finely chopped
1 garlic clove, crushed
juice of 1 lime
300 g (11 oz) cooked peeled prawns
2 tablespoons chopped fresh
  coriander
few drops of Tabasco
1 ripe avocado
½ iceberg lettuce, shredded
salt and freshly ground black pepper

This lighter version of the traditional prawn cocktail is reminiscent of Mexican *ceviche*, which is raw fish marinated in lime juice and chilli. It can be served as a light lunch or a starter.

▸ Place the tomatoes in a large bowl. Add the spring onions, chilli, garlic and lime juice. Stir to combine. Add the prawns, coriander and Tabasco and season well. Stir again and set aside to marinate for 10 minutes.
▸ Halve, stone and peel the avocado, dice the flesh and stir it gently into the prawn mixture. Arrange a handful of lettuce on each plate, spoon the prawn cocktail over and serve immediately.

Flash-fried goats' cheese with grape and chilli chutney

Serves 2 as a light lunch
or 4 as a starter
Preparation 10 mins
Cooking 15 mins
2 shallots
1 mild red chilli
1 tablespoon olive oil
250 g (9 oz) seedless red grapes
4 tablespoons golden caster sugar
2 tablespoons red wine vinegar
2 heads chicory
handful of frissee lettuce
2–3 tablespoons **Shallot vinaigrette**
  (page 185)
2 x 100g goats' cheeses

There are so many varieties of goats' cheeses, their flavours ranging from fresh and nutty to creamy, tangy or strong. Chevres, as the cheeses are called in France, are the best, but you can also get great goats' cheese made in Britain, Spain, Norway and North America. I like the stronger flavoured goats' cheese such as the Pouligny St Pierre, but if you prefer a mild taste, try Selles sur Cher. To enjoy the cheese at its best, eat within a few days of purchasing, except for the matured varieties. You need no oil when pan-frying these as you want to create a crust.

▸ Prepare the chutney first. Peel and slice the shallots and de-seed and finely chop the chilli. Heat the olive oil in a small pan, add the shallots and chilli and cook over a low-medium heat for about 2 minutes until tender but not coloured. Add the grapes, sugar and vinegar and continue to cook over a low heat for about 10 minutes until the chutney has thickened to a jam-like consistency. Remove from the heat and set aside while you prepare the salad and cook the goats' cheese.
▸ Separate the leaves from the chicory and mix in a bowl with the frissee. Toss in the dressing and arrange the salad on serving plates.
▸ Heat a non-stick frying pan over a medium heat. Remove the rind in a thin slice from both ends of each goats' cheese. Slice each of the cheeses into 2 discs and cook in the hot frying pan for about 30 seconds on each side until golden brown and bubbling.
▸ Arrange the hot cheese slices over the salad and add a good spoonful of the chutney. Serve immediately with some grilled sourdough bread.

Smoked haddock chowder

A speciality of New England, chowder is a thick soup that often incorporates seafood. But whether you use fish, clams or even fresh sweetcorn, it makes a fabulous hearty meal, especially on a blustery winter's day. To make it grander, add prawns or cooked mussels.

▸ Melt the butter in a large pan over a low to medium heat, add the onion, leeks and bacon and cook for about 5 minutes until tender.
▸ Peel and dice the potatoes. Add to the pan with the stock and some seasoning. Cover and bring to the boil. Reduce the heat and simmer gently for about 10–15 minutes, until the potatoes are tender.
▸ Meanwhile, cook the haddock. Place in a large frying pan, add the milk and bay leaf and bring to the boil. Cover and simmer gently for about 5 minutes, until the fish is cooked through. Remove from the pan with a fish slice and flake into chunks, removing any skin and bones.
▸ Strain the fish milk into the soup and add the haddock and sweetcorn. Simmer for a further minute, scatter with the parsley and serve in warm bowls with crusty bread and unsalted butter.

Serves 4
Preparation 5 mins
Cooking 20 mims
25 g (1 oz) butter
1 onion, chopped
2 leeks, sliced
4 rashers smoked streaky bacon, diced
450 g (1 lb) floury potatoes
450 ml (3/4 pint) fish or vegetable stock
450 g (1 lb) smoked haddock
450 ml (3/4 pint) milk
1 bay leaf
1 x 195-g (7-oz) can sweetcorn kernels, drained
2 tablespoons roughly chopped fresh parsley
salt and freshly ground black pepper

Good for winter warming
It's so important to eat well in the cold winter months to boost the body's strength. If you've been out for the day with friends and family, it's great to come in from the wet and cold and tuck into this rewarding chowder.

Substantial salads

Chargrilled vegetables with pan-seared goats' cheese and walnut and basil dressing

Serves 6
Preparation 10 mins
Cooking 30 mins
1 red pepper
1 yellow pepper
2 medium aubergines
4 tablespoons olive oil
2 courgettes
1 red onion
200 g (7 oz) chargrilled artichoke hearts in olive oil, drained
3 x 75-g (3-oz) goats' cheeses
salt and freshly ground black pepper

Walnut and basil dressing
1 garlic clove, crushed
50 g (2 oz) toasted walnuts
5 tablespoons extra-virgin olive oil
2 tablespoons roughly chopped fresh basil
1 tablespoon roughly chopped fresh flatleaf parsley

Good for your figure
Using a grill is the ultimate low-fat cooking method – you get a tempting explosion of smoky flavours as the dry heat of the fire melts away the fat.

Charring on a hot griddle brings out the juices and sugars in the vegetables, giving them that distinctive smell and flavour. You can do this on the barbie or indoors: just turn on the extractor fan as it can get a little smoky.

To save time, you could use roasted peppers from a jar. English goats' cheese with a thin rind is ideal for this recipe.

▸ Preheat a ridged griddle pan. Cut the peppers into quarters, remove the cores and seeds and grill skin-side down on the griddle until the skin is charred and blistered. Place in a bowl, cover with cling film and set aside. The peppers will steam and you will be able to remove the skins more easily.
▸ Slice the aubergines into discs no thicker than 1 cm (½ inch). Brush with a little of the olive oil and cook on the griddle pan until nicely browned on both sides with criss-cross griddle marks. Transfer to a large plate.
▸ Cut the courgettes into long slices (using a peeler with a bit of pressure when cutting will give you a good enough thickness). Brush the slices with oil and grill in the same way as the aubergines. Cut the onion into 1-cm (½-inch) discs, keeping the rings together: this makes cooking easier. Brush with oil and grill on both sides until tender and browned. Add the courgettes and onion to the aubergines.
▸ Make the dressing. Tip all the dressing ingredients into a blender, season well and mix until almost smooth.
▸ Peel the charred skin from the peppers and thickly slice the flesh. Add to all the other veggies along with the artichokes. Season, pour over the dressing and gently mix together using your hands. Divide between plates.
▸ Heat a non-stick frying pan over a medium heat. Slice each goats' cheese into two discs and cook in the hot frying pan for about 30 seconds on each side, until golden brown and bubbling. Arrange a slice top of each portion of the chargrilled vegetables and serve immediately with crusty bread.

Tuna, three-tomato and three-bean salad

Here's a salad that's packed full of flavour and protein. It makes an ideal lunch, or you can serve it as a starter for eight people with half a soft-boiled egg on top of each portion.

▸ Halve the large tomatoes, remove the cores, cut into wedges and place in a large bowl. Halve the cherry tomatoes, and roughly chop the sun-blushed tomatoes. Add them to the bowl and mix them with the large tomatoes.

▸ Bring a pan of salted water to the boil, add the fine green beans and broad beans and cook for about 3 minutes, until tender. Drain and refresh under cold running water. Pat dry on kitchen paper, then mix together in a large bowl with the cannellini beans.

▸ Make the dressing. Whisk the vinegar, oil and sugar together and season well. Pour half the dressing over the tomatoes and half over the beans; mix gently.

▸ Arrange a small handful of rocket in four bowls and top with the mixed beans, tuna, tomatoes and olives. Scatter with the basil and serve immediately.

Quick tip
Tinned tuna is a great way of working protein into any meal in minutes. Use best-quality tuna in extra-virgin olive oil.

Serves 4
Preparation 15 mins
Cooking 3 mins
4 large, ripe tomatoes
225 g (8 oz) mixed red and yellow cherry tomatoes
75 g (3 oz) sun-blushed or sun-dried tomatoes
150 g (5 oz) fine green beans, trimmed
150 g (5 oz) podded broad beans
1 x 400-g (14-oz) can cannellini beans, drained and rinsed
150 g (5 oz) tinned tuna in extra-virgin olive oil, drained and flaked

Dressing
1 tablespoon balsamic vinegar
3 tablespoons extra-virgin olive oil
½ teaspoon soft light brown sugar
salt and freshly ground black pepper

To serve
50 g (2 oz) wild rocket
2 tablespoons pitted black olives, roughly chopped
25 g (1 oz) fresh basil, shredded

Roquefort, apple and walnut salad

Serves 4
Preparation 10 mins
Cooking none
2 Braeburn apples
juice of ½ lemon
6 spring onions, trimmed
150 g (5 oz) raw beetroot

Dressing
1 teaspoon wholegrain mustard
1 tablespoon white wine or cider
   vinegar
4 tablespoons extra-virgin olive oil
1 teaspoon clear honey
salt and freshly ground black pepper

To serve
150 g (5 oz) mixed watercress and
   wild rocket
75 g (3 oz) toasted walnuts
100 g (4 oz) Roquefort, crumbled
25 g (1 oz) pecorino shavings

Toasting the walnuts brings out the natural oils, makes them crisper and intensifies the flavour. Any crumbly cheese – Stilton, feta, Cheshire or Lancashire – can go with this salad, but for me the semi-soft Roquefort wins every time.

Wear gloves to prevent the beetroot staining your hands, or use cling film to hold it. Walnut oil can be used in place of extra-virgin olive oil.

▸ Quarter, core and slice the apples. Toss in the lemon juice to prevent them discolouring. Thinly slice the spring onions on the diagonal. Peel the beetroot, then cut it into fine matchsticks or grate coarsely.
▸ Make the dressing. Place the mustard, vinegar, oil and honey in a small bowl, add seasoning and whisk until combined.
▸ Place a handful of watercress and rocket leaves in four bowls and arrange the apples, spring onions and beetroot on top. Scatter with the walnuts and Roquefort. Drizzle with the dressing, top with the pecorino and serve immediately with crusty bread.

Fresh and fabulous shopping

Good cooking starts with good shopping. Always look for the freshest, best-quality ingredients, and get to know the speciality stores in your area that can offer you something different. Markets, delis and organic retailers have really become a part of modern-day life. Supermarkets are now offering a much wider range of ingredients, but it's nice to make the effort and visit the smaller local shops and markets. It's one of the great ways we learn about other nationalities and cultures – long gone are the days when going to the Chinese restaurant was the only way of experiencing exotic foods of the world.

Farmers' markets

The real beauty of visiting a market is that wonderful personal service you get. I have fond memories of shopping down the Northcote Road in London with my mum and, although it's not as vibrant now, it still retains the personal attention that you somehow don't get in the supermarkets. Farmers' markets are a great opportunity to meet the people that actually produce the food you're buying, cooking and eating. As the farmers sell their produce directly to the public you can be sure that you are buying the best the season has to offer. Not only does this reduce the miles that your food has to travel before it reaches your kitchen, it also cuts down on needless plastic and packaging.

Delis

Check out your local Italian grocer for the best selection of olives, pasta, salamis and cheeses – perfect for a lazy supper without having to resort to a supermarket ready meal. But don't just rely on one grocer as there are a whole range of delis out there for you to choose from.

Organic greengrocers

As we all become more and more conscious of good-quality food, organic greengrocers are popping up all over the place. The produce can be a bit more 'rustic' but I have to say you can't beat a muddy carrot, spud or the odd apple with a meaty maggot!

'Real' butchers and fishmongers

I'm glad to say that as our demand for quality produce increases, local traders are becoming popular once again. Make friends with your nearest butcher so that you can benefit from their valuable knowledge and cooking tips. Meat from a quality butchers is outstanding – there really is no comparison to that stuff you buy in the cellophane packets at supermarkets! And the sheer variety on offer makes the fishmongers worth a visit.

Chicken, prawn, mango and avocado salad with ginger lime dressing

This delightful salad looks great on the plate and is a joy to eat.
Avocado is a fruit rather than a vegetable, and was once called the
butter pear because of its creamy consistency. It's used mainly in salads
because the flavour is very subtle – some might even say bland. Not me,
though – I love it.

Avocado oil is now available in some supermarkets and most health
food shops. For a tropical touch add some chopped fresh papaya to
the salad.

▸ Make the dressing first. Place the lime zest in a small bowl, add
1 tablespoon of the lime juice and the vinegar, ginger and oil, then
season and mix to combine.
▸ Cut the chicken into bite-size pieces. Place in a bowl and add the prawns.
Peel the mango and cut the cheeks away from the stone. Cut the flesh into
chunks and add to the bowl. Cut the avocado in half, discard the stone and
skin, then thickly slice the flesh into the bowl along with the cucumber.
▸ Arrange the lettuce leaves on four plates and top with the chicken
mixture. Drizzle with the dressing, then scatter with the cashew nuts
and basil. Serve immediately.

Serves 4
Preparation 15 mins
Cooking none
2 cooked chicken breasts, skinned
   and cooled
200 g (7 oz) cooked, peeled king
   prawns
1 ripe mango
1 ripe avocado
¼ cucumber, peeled and sliced
4 gem lettuces, leaves separated
100 g (4 oz) toasted cashews
handful of fresh small basil leaves

Ginger lime dressing
zest and juice of 1 lime
2 teaspoons white wine vinegar
½ teaspoon grated fresh ginger
3 tablespoons avocado oil or extra-
   virgin olive oil
salt and freshly ground black pepper

Good for your skin
Avocado is rich in oils, proteins
and vitamins: no wonder it's
used in skincare products.

Chargrilled steak, asparagus and warm potato salad with salsa verde

Steak and potato salad? Yes, please. Although I've recommended
fillet or sirloin, you could use a large forerib fillet (rib-eye) and divide
it between the salads. Authentic salsa verde contains anchovies, but
leave them out if they're not your bag. Remember to be easy on the
salt if you do keep them in.

▸ Wash the potatoes and cook in boiling salted water until tender.
▸ Meanwhile, make the salsa verde. Place all the ingredients in the
bowl of a food processor. Season and blend until finely chopped and
amalgamated: this takes only 5–10 seconds.
▸ Drain the potatoes and cool slightly. Cut into 1-cm (½-inch) slices
and place in a large bowl. Add the onion and salsa verde and toss.
▸ Heat a ridged griddle pan and turn on the extractor fan as it will get
a little smoky. Season the steaks, brush with a little oil and grill for about
3–4 minutes on each side for medium-rare. Remove from the pan and rest
the meat for 5 minutes. Meanwhile, toss the asparagus in a little more oil
and cook on the griddle for 5–6 minutes, until nicely charred and tender.
▸ Divide the potato salad between four plates and arrange the asparagus
on top. Thinly slice the steaks across the grain and arrange on top of the
salad. Scatter with the capers and serve immediately.

Serves 4
Preparation 10 mins
Cooking 30 mins
500g (1 lb 2 oz) waxy new potatoes
1 red onion, sliced
2 x 175-g (6-oz) fillet or sirloin steaks
olive
 for grilling
250 g (9 oz) bunch asparagus,
   trimmed
1 tablespoon capers, rinsed
salt and freshly ground black pepper

Salsa verde
1 garlic clove, crushed
25 g (1 oz) wild rocket or watercress
   (optional)
20 g (¾ oz) bunch fresh flatleaf
   parsley
juice of ½ lemon
2 teaspoons Dijon mustard
4 tablespoons extra-virgin olive oil
4 anchovy fillets (optional)

◐ Super-quick recipe
Fennel, pear and Parma ham salad

Serves 4
Preparation 10 mins
Cooking none
1 large head fennel
2 ripe pears
juice of ½ lemon
1 red onion
150 g (5 oz) dolcelatte cheese
2 heads radicchio
handful of wild rocket
handful of curly endive
12 slices Parma ham or bresaola
100 g (4 oz) toasted hazelnuts,
   roughly chopped
50 g (2 oz) Parmesan shavings
   (optional)
salt and freshly ground black pepper

Dressing
4 tablespoons walnut or hazelnut oil
1 tablespoon sherry vinegar
1 small shallot, finely diced
1 teaspoon clear honey

Wasn't fennel the thing we thought was an overdose of onion in salads way back when? How wrong we were. Sliced thinly and eaten raw, baked in a little stock for half an hour, or gently poached in sugar syrup and glazed, fennel is always delicious. This crunchy salad really captures its bittersweet taste, and ripe, flavoursome pear is a great contrast: I recommend the red-skinned variety Red Bartlett. Bresaola can be used instead of Parma ham. If you wish, you could keep the aniseedy fronds (dill weed) from the top of the fennel, and chop them up later and add to the salad.

▸ Make the dressing first. Combine all the ingredients in a small bowl, add seasoning and whisk to combine.
▸ Trim the fennel and slice it as thinly as possible, using a mandolin or the thin setting on your food processor (yes, the one you never use); otherwise it's a sharp knife by hand. Quarter and core the pears, slice thinly and toss in the lemon juice to prevent them discolouring. Slice the onion as thinly as you can. Add both to the fennel, crumble in the dolcelatte and toss lightly with your hands.
▸ Arrange the radicchio, rocket and endive on four plates. Pile the fennel salad on top, then tear the Parma ham into pieces and drape them over the salad. Scatter with the hazelnuts and drizzle with the dressing. Top with the Parmesan shavings (if using) and serve immediately.

Hot-smoked salmon with avocado and pink grapefruit salad

This tangy, refreshing salad uses trendy hot-smoked salmon, which most good supermarkets and many delis are now selling. It's really delicious and quite different from the usual smoked salmon as you buy it as a whole fillet instead of thin slices.

The sharp but not too sour flavour of the grapefruit marries well with all types of smoked fish: you could use smoked mackerel or trout with this recipe. Choose a grapefruit that is heavy for its size – a sign of juiciness – and has a good plump skin.

▸ Peel the grapefruit by cutting a slice from the top of the fruit to expose the flesh, then remove the skin as you would peel an apple, cutting just beneath the white pith. Hold the peeled fruit in the palm of your hand and carefully cut out each segment between the thin lines of pith. Do this over a bowl so that you can catch all the juices.

▸ Cut the onion in half, remove the root with an angled knife and slice as finely as possible. Cut the avocados in half, discard the stones and skin, then slice or cube the flesh. Add to the grapefruit along with the onion.

▸ To make the dressing, whisk the mustard, vinegar and oil together in a small bowl and season well.

▸ Trim the stalks from the chicory, separate the leaves and arrange on four plates. Put the grapefruit mixture on top then flake the salmon and scatter it over each of the salads.

▸ Drizzle with the dressing, top with the pecans and parsley and serve immediately.

Serves 4
Preparation 10 mins
Cooking none
2 pink or ruby grapefruit
1 small red onion
2 avocados
4 heads mixed red and white chicory
150 g (5 oz) hot-smoked salmon

Dressing
1 teaspoon Dijon mustard
1 tablespoon white wine vinegar
3 tablespoons extra-virgin olive oil
  or avocado oil
salt and freshly ground black pepper

To serve
50 g (2 oz) toasted pecans, roughly
  chopped
2 tablespoons roughly chopped fresh
  flatleaf parsley

Good for colour
Who could resist the stunning ruby flesh of a ripe grapefruit? Mix vibrant reds and greens in salads to create a visual delight.

Vietnamese-style crispy pork and little gem salad

Serves 4
Preparation 10 mins
Cooking 10 mins

1 tablespoon sunflower oil
450 g (1 lb) pork mince
2 teaspoons freshly grated ginger
1 red chilli, seeded and finely chopped
1 garlic clove, crushed
4 spring onions, trimmed
2 tablespoons chopped fresh coriander
2 tablespoons chopped fresh mint
2 teaspoons soy sauce
2 tablespoons fish sauce
2 tablespoons rice vinegar or white wine vinegar
1 teaspoon soft light brown sugar
3 limes
50 g (2 oz) dry-roasted peanuts, chopped
4 little gem lettuces
fresh coriander sprigs, to serve

If you've never tried this type of salad before, please do as I'm sure it will become a favourite. When cooking the meat, make sure you fry it for a long enough time to achieve the necessary crispiness.

This recipe also works well with minced chicken, and the filled leaves make great canapés.

▸ Heat half the oil in a large frying pan over a high heat. Add half the pork and cook, stirring occasionally, until browned and crispy. Remove from the pan and put into a bowl or dish, then cook the remaining mince in the same way.
▸ In another bowl mix together the ginger, chilli and garlic. Finely slice the spring onions and add to the bowl with the herbs. Add the soy sauce, fish sauce, vinegar, sugar and the juice of 1 lime. Give it a good mix, then pour the mixture over the crispy pork. Scatter the peanuts over the mince.
▸ Cut the remaining limes into wedges and separate the leaves of the lettuces.
▸ Scoop some crispy mince on to each lettuce leaf, add a squeeze of lime, top with a sprig of coriander and serve.

Brown basmati and mottled bean salad

Serves 4–6
Preparation 15 mins
Cooking 20 mins

75 g (3 oz) brown basmati rice
100 g (4 oz) French beans, trimmed
1 x 410-g (14½-oz) can borlotti beans
1 small red onion
150 g (5 oz) cherry tomatoes
50 g (2 oz) sun-dried or sun-blushed tomatoes
150 g (5 oz) feta
2 tablespoons chopped parsley
1 tablespoon chopped mint

Dressing
juice of ½ lemon
3 tablespoons extra-virgin olive oil
1 teaspoon Dijon mustard
salt and freshly ground black pepper

Oval-shaped borlotti beans are often mottled in colour, hence the name of this recipe. They have a bittersweet flavour that works well in salads, pasta dishes and hearty Italian soups. This is a lovely vegetarian salad to take on a picnic.

▸ Cook the rice in boiling salted water for about 20 minutes, or until tender. Drain and rinse briefly under cold running water. Shake off all excess water.
▸ Cut the French beans into 2.5-cm (1-inch) lengths and cook in lightly salted boiling water for about 2 minutes, until tender. Refresh under cold water and pat dry with kitchen paper.
▸ Rinse the borlotti beans and drain well. Place in a large bowl and add the cooked rice and French beans. Finely chop the onion and halve the cherry tomatoes. Roughly chop the sun-dried or sun-blushed tomatoes and crumble the feta. Add to the bowl along with the chopped herbs and mix lightly.
▸ To make the dressing, place the lemon juice, oil and mustard in a small bowl, season well and whisk together. Pour this over the salad, mix well and set aside for 30 minutes to allow the flavours to combine. Serve with crusty bread.

Serves 4
Preparation 10 mins
Cooking 3 mins
4 duck breasts, skinned
2 tablespoons sunflower oil
2 teaspoons Chinese five-spice
  powder
1 tablespoon toasted sesame seeds,
  to serve

Vegetable salad
2 carrots
1/4 cucumber, seeded
50 g (2 oz) mangetout, trimmed
2 spring onions, trimmed
1/4 head Chinese leaves
50 g (2 oz) bean sprouts, rinsed

Dressing
2 tablespoons olive oil
1 teaspoon sesame oil
1 tablespoon light soy sauce
1 tablespoon rice vinegar
1 red chilli, seeded and finely
  chopped
pinch of caster sugar

● Super-quick recipe
Warm five-spiced duck and crisp vegetable salad

This salad brings lots of oriental flavours harmoniously together.
There are several duck varieties on the market today, including
Aylesbury and Gressingham, which are British and known for their
flavour and texture. The French prefer to use Barbary or Muscovy
ducks as they have a stronger flavour.

▸ Slice the duck breasts into 1-cm (1/2-inch) strips, pop into a bowl and
mix with 1 tablespoon of the oil and five-spice powder. Set aside while
you prepare the salad.
▸ Peel the carrots, then continue to peel off carrot ribbons. Cut the
cucumber and mangetout into fine matchsticks. Trim the spring onions
and Chinese leaves and shred as finely as you can. Place the prepared
vegetables in a bowl and add the bean sprouts.
▸ Mix all the dressing ingredients together in a large bowl.
▸ Place the rest of the oil in a wok or frying pan over a high heat until
almost smoking. Add the duck strips and stir-fry for 2–3 minutes, until
nicely brown but still a little pink in the middle. Add to the dressing
and mix well.
▸ Arrange the salad on plates, then spoon the succulent duck and
dressing on top. Scatter with toasted sesame seeds and serve
immediately.

Quick tip
Ask your local butcher to prepare
your meat for you in advance.
Boneless, skinless breasts are needed
for this recipe.

Bang-bang chicken with vegetable ribbon salad

I first tried this dish many moons ago at Le Caprice, the famous London restaurant that originally brought it to people's attention, and where it's a favourite to this day.

   If you'd like to poach rather than roast the chicken breasts, cover them with water and add some sliced onion, garlic, fresh ginger and a few peppercorns. The resulting stock can be used to make a lovely soup.

▸ Make the dressing first. Place all the ingredients in a glass bowl that will fit snugly on top of a small pan of simmering water. Do not allow the bottom of the bowl to touch the water. Stir until the dressing is smooth. Remove from the heat and keep warm.

▸ Using a vegetable peeler, cut the cucumber and carrots into long ribbons. Slice the spring onions. Mix together the cucumber, carrots, spring onions and bean sprouts. Divide the salad between four plates. Shred the chicken and arrange on top of the salad. Drizzle with the dressing, scatter with the peanuts and sesame seeds (if using) and serve immediately with any extra dressing served alongside.

Serves 4
Preparation 15 mins
Cooking none

1 cucumber
3 medium carrots, peeled
4 spring onions, trimmed
50 g (2 oz) bean sprouts, rinsed
4 cooked chicken breasts, cooled
75 g (3 oz) dry-roasted peanuts, chopped
1 tablespoon toasted sesame seeds (optional)

Dressing
100 g (4 oz) smooth peanut butter
3 tablespoons sesame oil
2 tablespoons sunflower or groundnut oil
2 tablespoons chilli sauce
1 tablespoon soy sauce
1 tablespoon rice vinegar or lime juice
1 garlic clove, crushed

Good for your budget
Chicken is so versatile that it makes sense to put any leftovers to good use. Create some healthy sandwiches for lunch and then use the stock to make a nutritious soup.

The other Greek salad

While the family and I were holidaying in Greece, I noticed that this simple crisp salad often popped up as a side dish to our meal. It was a welcome change from the usual feta salad with tomatoes and olives. The Greeks call it *maroulosalata*, and it has a crunchy zing that goes well with grilled meats and oily fish. Add the dressing just before serving or the acidity of the vinegar will make the lettuce go soggy. I've added a few nuts to the formula, but you can leave them out if you wish.

▶ Roughly shred the lettuce and place in a large bowl. Trim and roughly chop the spring onions. Add to the lettuce with the dill.

▶ In a small bowl mix whisk together the oil and vinegar or lemon juice, then season well.

▶ Pour the dressing over the salad, add the nuts or seeds and toss together. Serve immediately.

Serves 4–6
Preparation 5 mins
Cooking none
1 cos lettuce
6 spring onions
2 tablespoons roughly chopped fresh dill
5 tablespoons extra-virgin olive oil
2 tablespoons white wine vinegar or lemon juice
1 tablespoon toasted flaked almonds, sunflower seeds, or sesame seeds
salt and freshly ground black pepper

Quick and easy suppers

Gr8 steak and mushroom sandwiches

Serves 2
Preparation 5 mins
Cooking 15 mins
3 tablespoons olive oil
1 red onion, sliced
1 garlic clove, crushed
1 tablespoon balsamic vinegar
2 large or 4 medium-sized flat
   mushrooms, stalks trimmed
2 x 150-g (5-oz) rump or sirloin
   steaks, trimmed of excess fat
2 x 15-cm (6-inch) pieces
   French bread
2 tablespoons Dijon mustard
handful of wild rocket or fresh
   flatleaf parsley leaves
salt and freshly ground black pepper

Good for feeding your mates

Steak is simple, honest, fun food that never fails to hit the spot. You can guarantee that somewhere in the world right now, a group of friends are enjoying great conversation over a great steak sarnie.

We just seem to love sandwiches in Britain, and for me the secret is in the bread. I'd get this sandwich ready for my mates after a late night at the Comedy Store, where I used to perform in a double act called the Calypso Twins. They were fun times and, being young, I could do two jobs – one in the kitchen and the other on stage. Perhaps that's why I love doing *Ready Steady Cook*.

You need thin steaks for this – ask the butcher to slice them no thicker than 1 cm (½ inch).

These sandwiches are delicious cold, when all the juices have soaked into the bread, but they can also be eaten hot.

▸ Heat 2 tablespoons of the oil in a frying pan, add the onion and sauté over a medium heat until tender and turning golden at the edges. Add the garlic and cook for 30 seconds. Add the vinegar and cook for another minute. Tip the onions on to a plate while you cook the mushrooms.
▸ Wipe the mushrooms with damp kitchen paper. Add the remaining tablespoon of oil to the pan and cook the mushrooms on both sides for about 5 minutes, until tender. Remove from the pan.
▸ Season the steaks and cook in the frying pan over a high heat for about 1½ minutes on each side for medium, or until cooked to your liking.
▸ Cut each piece of bread almost in half and spread liberally with 1 tablespoon of the mustard. Place a steak on the bottom half and pile half the onion on top, followed by half the mushrooms. Scatter with rocket or parsley, add seasoning and press the sandwich together.
▸ Wrap the sandwiches tightly in greaseproof paper, and eat when cold with gherkins and plenty of napkins.

Roasted vegetable wraps with hummus and goats' cheese

What would we do without the old sandwich, roll and wrap, eh?
We love them all, from BLTs to submarines. Mediterranean wraps are everywhere now, but pitta breads or even toasted ciabatta rolls work well.

The mild, spreadable goats' cheese that comes in tubs is the best one to use, but a flavoursome cream cheese will do instead.

▸ Preheat a ridged griddle pan, or an ordinary grill.
▸ Cut the aubergine and courgettes into slices on the diaganol no thicker than 1 cm (½ inch). Brush with a little oil and cook on the griddle pan or under the grill until nicely criss-crossed or browned on both sides. Transfer to a large plate to cool.
▸ Warm the wraps on the griddle pan or under the grill, then place on a work surface. Spoon 1 tablespoon of the goats' cheese on to each wrap, spreading it almost to the edges. Top with a quarter of the chargrilled vegetables and 1 tablespoon of the roasted peppers (if using). Season well.
▸ Roughly spread the hummus over the vegetables, add some rocket or spinach leaves and scatter with the pine nuts. Roll up each wrap, completely encasing the filling. Tightly wrap in foil, twisting the ends. Remove from the foil and cut the wraps diagonally when ready to serve.

Makes 4
Preparation 10 mins
Cooking 15 mins
1 medium aubergine
2 courgettes
2–3 tablespoons olive oil
4 Mediterranean wraps
4 tablespoons spreadable
  goats' cheese
4 tablespoons roughly chopped
  roasted peppers (optional)
4 tablespoons hummus
handful of wild rocket or young
  leaf spinach
50 g (2 oz) toasted pine nuts
salt and freshly ground black pepper

Teatime pasta with sausage sauce

When the kids get home from after-school sports feeling ravenous,
and you've had a busy day, a quick, tasty pasta dish with familiar ingredients always delivers.

You can use either fresh or bottled tomato sauce in this recipe, and feel free to use one that contains extra veggies. If you want to jazz things up for the adults at a casual supper party, use prawns in place of sausages, and get hold of some Cassarecce pasta, available from good supermarkets and delis.

▸ Heat the oil in a large frying pan. Add the pepper, onion, chilli and oregano and cook over a medium heat, stirring occasionally, until the onion is soft but not coloured. Add the garlic and continue to cook for a further minute.
▸ Add the sausages to the pan, breaking up the meat with a wooden spoon. Cook until well browned, then pour in the tomato sauce. Season and continue to cook gently for a further 10 minutes. For adults you can add a splash of wine here if you like.
▸ Meanwhile, cook the pasta in a large pan of boiling salted water according to the packet instructions. Drain and mix thoroughly with the sausage sauce. Scatter with the basil and Parmesan, and serve immediately.

Serves 4
Preparation 5 mins
Cooking 20 mins
1 tablespoon olive oil
1 red pepper, seeded and diced
1 onion, finely chopped
pinch of crushed dried chilli
  (optional)
pinch of dried oregano
1 garlic clove, crushed
400 g (14 oz) good-quality sausages,
  skinned
350 g (12 oz) tomato pasta sauce
300–400 g (11–14 oz) penne pasta
1 tablespoon chopped fresh basil
freshly grated Parmesan, to serve
salt and freshly ground black pepper

Chicken, ham and mushroom crusty puff pies

Serves 4
Preparation 10 mins
Cooking 30 mins

150 g (5 oz) button mushrooms
25 g (1 oz) butter
4 skinless, cooked chicken breasts
100 g (4 oz) lean ham
350 g (12 oz) fresh or ready-made
  cheese sauce
100 g (4 oz) frozen peas
1 tablespoon chopped fresh parsley
  or tarragon
300 g (11 oz) puff pastry
1 tablespoon plain flour, for dusting
2 tablespoons milk
salt and freshly ground black pepper

I'm always disappointed and sometimes frustrated when I taste shop-bought pies because the meat is invariably thin and stringy and the pastry all too often soggy. So here's a lovely, moist pie that has bite and light, crisp pastry.

If pushed for time, you could use a ready-made carbonara sauce or cheese and mushroom sauce.

▸ Preheat the oven to 200°C/400°F/Gas mark 6.
▸ Thickly slice the mushrooms. Melt the butter in a frying pan, add the mushrooms and sauté over a medium to high heat for 3–4 minutes, until tender. Tip into a large bowl.
▸ Cut the chicken into chunks and roughly chop the ham. Pour the sauce over the mushrooms, add the chicken, ham, peas and parsley or tarragon. Season, mix well and divide between 4 individual pie dishes. Brush the edges of each dish with a little cold water.
▸ Lightly dust a work surface with the flour, roll the pastry out and cut out four discs slightly larger than the pie dishes. Cover the dishes with the pastry discs, pressing down the edges to seal. Cut a hole for the steam to escape. Brush the tops with the milk, then place the dishes on a baking sheet and cook on the middle shelf of the oven for about 20 minutes, until the pies are piping hot and golden brown. Serve immediately with steamed broccoli.

Penne with roasted cherry tomato and melting taleggio sauce

Serves 4
Preparation 10 mins
Cooking 25 mins

400 g (14 oz) cherry tomatoes
3 tablespoons extra-virgin olive oil,
  or use the oil from the sun-dried
  tomatoes
2 garlic cloves, sliced
pinch of crushed dried chilli
350–400 g (12–14 oz) penne pasta
2 shallots, sliced
6 sun-dried tomatoes, drained
2 tablespoons roughly chopped
  black olives
1 x 20-g (¾-oz) packet fresh basil,
  leaves shredded
50 g (2 oz) wild rocket or watercress
75 g (3 oz) taleggio, diced
salt and freshly ground black pepper
Parmesan shavings, to serve

Ready-made sauces are great to have on standby, but they are vastly improved by a few additions here and there. If you don't like anything too spicy, use a plain tomato sauce rather than an arrabiata one. Of course, the sauce in this recipe is best of all. *Bellissimo!*

▸ Preheat the oven to 200°C/400°F/Gas mark 6.
▸ Toss the cherry tomatoes in half the oil, then add the garlic and chilli. Place in a small roasting tray and cook on the middle shelf of the oven for 15–20 minutes.
▸ Bring a large pan of salted water to the boil and cook the pasta according to the packet instructions. Heat the remaining oil in a saucepan, add the shallots and cook for a few minutes, until beginning to colour.
▸ Cut the sun-dried tomatoes into slivers, add to the shallots and cook for 1 minute. Add the olives, roasted cherry tomatoes, basil, wild rocket or watercress and taleggio. Cook for a further 20 seconds to start the cheese melting.
▸ Drain the pasta and gently stir in the tomato mixture. Season and serve in warm bowls with Parmesan shavings scattered on top.

Thai-style chicken, corn and prawn cakes with sweet chilli sauce

As my wife says, these are simply delicious and so easy to prepare. The curry paste quantity is approximate, depending on how spicy you like your food: 1 tablespoon = mild, 3 tablespoons = hot.

▸ Roughly chop the chicken breasts and place in the bowl of a food processor. Add the prawns, egg white, garlic and curry paste. Process until finely chopped. Tip into a bowl, add the breadcrumbs, sweetcorn, coriander and spring onions, and mix until well combined. Using wet hands, shape the mixture into approximately 16 small patties.
▸ To make the sweet chilli sauce, mix the three sauces together, add the cucumber (if using) and set aside.
▸ Heat the oil in a large frying pan. Add the patties a few at a time and cook for about 1–2 minutes on each side, until golden brown. Drain on kitchen paper and serve with lime wedges and the sweet chilli sauce.

Quick tip
If you're using a food processor, make the breadcrumbs in it before you blitz the chicken – it saves on the washing-up.

**Serves 4 as a main course
and 6 as a starter
Preparation 10 mins
Cooking 10 mins**
2 skinless chicken breasts
250 g (9 oz) raw tiger prawns, peeled and deveined
1 egg white
1 garlic clove, crushed
1–3 tablespoons Thai red curry paste
50 g (2 oz) fresh breadcrumbs
1 x 195-g (7-oz) can sweetcorn, drained
2 tablespoons chopped fresh coriander
4 spring onions, sliced
2 tablespoons sunflower oil
1 lime, cut into wedges, to serve

Sweet chilli sauce
4 tablespoons sweet chilli sauce
1 teaspoon soy sauce
1 teaspoon fish sauce
5-cm (2-inch) piece cucumber, peeled, seeded and finely chopped (optional)

Green crunchy vegetable stir-fry with cashews and black bean sauce

Serves 4
Preparation 5 mins
Cooking 6 mins

1 onion
1 red or green chilli (optional)
1 garlic clove
2 courgettes
250 g (9 oz) asparagus, trimmed
3 spring onions, trimmed
2 tablespoons sunflower or
   groundnut oil
100 g (4 oz) sugarsnaps or
   mangetout, trimmed
225 g (8 oz) small broccoli florets
3–4 tablespoons black bean sauce
1 tablespoon chopped fresh
   coriander
50 g (2 oz) toasted unsalted cashews

Good for a daily dose of greens

All sorts of green veg work well in this recipe. So there's no excuse – throw in as much as you can!

This sounds healthy and tastes even better. The veggies I've listed are only a guideline, so feel free to use whatever is seasonal and available. You can't go wrong.

▸ Prepare all the vegetables before starting to cook. Slice the onion. If using the chilli, cut it in half lengthways, scrape out the seeds with a teaspoon and finely slice the flesh. Crush the garlic. Cut the courgettes in half lengthways, and cut each half diagonally into 1-cm (½-inch) slices. Cut the asparagus into 2.5-cm (1-inch) lengths. Finely slice the spring onions.
▸ Turn on the extractor fan and heat the oil in a wok. When hot, add the chilli (if using), garlic and three-quarters of the spring onions and stir-fry over a medium to high heat for 2 minutes.
▸ Add the courgettes, asparagus, onion, sugarsnaps or mangetout and broccoli. Continue to stir-fry for 4–5 minutes, until tender. Mix in the black bean sauce, evenly coating all the vegetables, and stir-fry for a further 30–60 seconds. Scatter with the coriander, the remaining spring onions and the cashews, and serve immediately with egg noodles or steamed rice.

Spaghetti with Sicilian cauliflower sauce

I first tasted something similar to this in the gorgeous city of Sydney, Australia. I can close my eyes and still taste it now. It really did bring my taste buds alive. Unfortunately, I didn't get the recipe, but this is my version and I hope you'll agree that it really is a mouthwatering experience.

To yield 450g (1 lb) of saffron a quarter of a million flowers have to be harvested by hand: that's probably why it's the most expensive spice in the world. But for a few pounds you can buy a sachet in your supermarket or deli, and believe me – it's worth every penny.

▸ Bring a large pan of salted water to the boil, add the cauliflower and cook for about 4 minutes. Place the saffron threads (if using) in a small bowl, cover with 1 tablespoon boiling water and set aside to soak for 5 minutes.

▸ Heat the oil in a large sauté pan. Add the onion and cook over a medium heat until tender but not coloured. Add the garlic and anchovy fillets and cook for a minute until the anchovies have 'melted'. Add the raisins and pine nuts and cook for 1 minute, until the pine nuts are lightly toasted.

▸ Using a slotted spoon, scoop the cauliflower out of the boiling water and add to the sauté pan. Stir in the saffron infusion (if using), tomato paste and 120 ml (4 fl oz) of the cauliflower water. Season and cook over a low to medium heat for about 5 minutes, whilst lightly breaking up the cauliflower with the back of a wooden spoon.

▸ Meanwhile, cook the spaghetti in the boiling cauliflower water according to the packet instructions. Drain well and tip the pasta into the sauté pan. Squeeze the lemon juice over, scatter with the parsley and mix gently to combine. Serve immediately with plenty of Parmesan to pass around.

Serves 4
Preparation 5 mins
Cooking 25 mins
1 medium cauliflower, cut into small florets
pinch of saffron threads
2 tablespoons extra-virgin olive oil
1 onion, chopped
2 garlic cloves, crushed
4 anchovy fillets in olive oil
50 g (2 oz) raisins
50 g (2 oz) pine nuts
2 tablespoons sun-dried tomato paste
400 g (14 oz) spaghetti
juice of ½ lemon
3 tablespoons chopped fresh flatleaf parsley
salt and freshly ground black pepper
freshly grated Parmesan, to serve

Good for a taste of the exotic
Saffron adds a delicate yet exquisite taste.

Salmon petals in Thai broth with rice noodles

Serves 2
Preparation 10 mins
Cooking 15 mins

1 stick lemon grass
2.5-cm (1-inch) piece fresh ginger
½ red chilli
900 ml (1½ pints) light fish or
    vegetable stock
1 lime leaf, fresh or dried
8 baby corn
50 g (2 oz) sugarsnaps
2 small heads pak choi
4 spring onions
1 tablespoon fish sauce
1 tablespoon soy sauce
2 x 150-g (5-oz) skinless, boneless
    salmon fillets
1 x 60-g (2¼-oz) bundle fine rice
    noodles
2 tablespoons chopped fresh
    coriander
lime wedges, to serve

When the salmon fillets are flaked, the pieces look just like pink petals, which creates a very pretty effect. For a more dramatic-looking dish, you could use peeled king prawns.

▸ Cut the lemon grass in half and crush slightly with a rolling pin. Peel and thinly slice the ginger. Seed and slice the chilli. Put the stock in a saucepan, add the lemon grass, ginger, chilli and lime leaf. Bring to the boil, then cover and simmer very gently for at least 5 minutes to allow the seasonings to infuse the stock.
▸ Prepare the vegetables for the broth. Cut the baby corn into thick diagonal slices and the sugarsnaps in half. Separate the pak choi leaves and cut any large ones in half. Trim and slice the spring onions diagonally. Set aside.
▸ Add the fish sauce and soy sauce to the stock. Lower the salmon fillets into the simmering stock, then cover and poach for about 5 minutes, or until just cooked through. Remove the fish from the pan and set aside.
▸ Strain the stock through a fine sieve into a clean pan. Bring back to the boil and add the baby corn and rice noodles. Simmer for 1 minute, add the sugarsnaps and pak choi and cook for a further minute. Gently flake the salmon into bite-size pieces and return to the broth with the spring onions.
▸ Divide the mixture between two warm bowls, scatter with the coriander and serve with lime wedges to squeeze over.

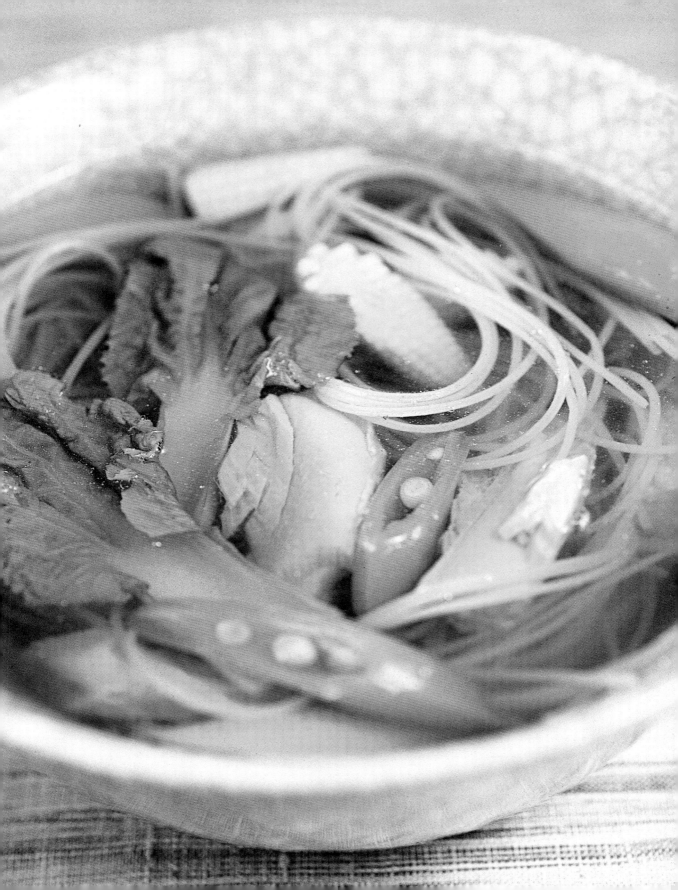

◖ Super-quick recipe
Smoked haddock rarebits

At last, it's easy to buy good haddock. For many years it seemed that the only smoked haddock available was dyed fluorescent yellow and chemically treated to taste of smoke. Now it's easy to pick out the good stuff because it's not dyed. Adding some crisp bacon at the end would be a nice touch, and gives an interesting combination of flavours.

▸ Place the haddock in a sauté pan and pour in the milk. Set over a medium heat and bring to the boil. Reduce the heat to a gentle simmer, cover and cook for about 5–6 minutes. Remove the fish from the pan and cool slightly before flaking into chunks.
▸ Preheat the grill and toast the bread on both sides.
▸ Mix the cheese sauce with the mustard, Worcestershire sauce and chives. Season, add the haddock and tomatoes, then fold together to combine, using a large metal spoon.
▸ Divide the cheesy fish mixture between the toasted bread, scatter with the Parmesan and place on a baking sheet. Cook under the grill until hot, bubbling and golden brown. Serve immediately with steamed spinach.

Serves 2
Preparation 10 mins
Cooking 5 mins
450–500 g (1 lb–1 lb 2 oz) smoked haddock fillet
250 ml (8 fl oz) milk
4 slices from a small white bloomer
1 x 350-g (12-oz) tub fresh cheese sauce
2 teaspoons Dijon or wholegrain mustard
splash of Worcestershire sauce
1 tablespoon snipped fresh chives
8 cherry tomatoes, halved
2 tablespoons freshly grated Parmesan
salt and freshly ground black pepper

Baked sardines with a peri-peri crust

Sardines can be a great addition to a tray of pre-dinner nibbles and peri-peri seasoning is sure to spice up any evening.

▸ Preheat the oven to 200°C/400°F/Gas mark 6.
▸ Tip the breadcrumbs on to a baking sheet and toast in the oven for about 4–5 minutes until golden. Remove from the oven and set aside to cool.
▸ Prepare the sardines. Cut the head off each one, slice through the belly and remove the guts. Place the sardine skin-side uppermost on a chopping board and press firmly down the length of the backbone. Turn the fish over and, using your fingers, pull the backbone and all the remaining bones away in one piece. Rinse the sardines under cold running water and pat dry with kitchen paper.
▸ Mix the breadcrumbs with the lemon zest, herbs and peri-peri seasoning. Season with salt and pepper.
▸ Dust the sardines with the flour and dip them into the beaten egg. Press them into the breadcrumbs and coat them thoroughly on all sides.
▸ Arrange the sardines on a baking sheet and cook in the oven for about 10 minutes until crisp and golden.
▸ Serve with lemon wedges and a good dollop of garlicky mayonnaise.

Serves 4
Preparation 15 mins
Cooking 15 mins
200 g (7 oz) fine fresh white breadcrumbs
8 sardines
grated zest of 1 unwaxed lemon
1 teaspoon chopped fresh thyme leaves
2 tablespoons finely chopped fresh parsley
4 teaspoons peri-peri seasoning
2–3 tablespoons plain flour
1 egg, beaten
salt and freshly ground black pepper
lemon wedges and garlicky mayonnaise, to serve

Chicken cordon bleu with lemon sage butter sauce

Serves 4
Preparation 10 mins
Cooking 10 mins
4 skinless chicken breasts
4 large slices prosciutto
100 g (4 oz) Gruyère cheese,
   thinly sliced
2 fresh sage leaves, roughly chopped
2 tablespoons plain flour
2 large eggs, beaten
175 g (6 oz) fresh white breadcrumbs
2 tablespoons olive oil
25 g (1 oz) butter
salt and freshly ground black pepper

Lemon sage butter sauce
50 g (2 oz) butter
4 fresh sage leaves, roughly chopped
juice of 1 small lemon

This classic dish can be made with chicken, veal or pork. Prosciutto ham is dry-cured, but don't let that stop you if you can't get hold of it: use ordinary cooked ham instead. The same applies to the cheese: Gruyère is great, but use anything that's knocking about in the fridge – Brie, Cheddar, Gorgonzola . . .

The sauce couldn't be easier: lemon and sage foaming in butter. Splash it generously over the chicken for a beautiful complementary taste.

It's worth buying a loaf of white bread, making a load of breadcrumbs and keeping them in the freezer in small bags to defrost and use at a moment's notice. Unsliced white sandwich bread makes the best breadcrumbs for coating.

▸ Preheat the oven to 200°C/400°F/Gas mark 6.
▸ Place each chicken breast between two large pieces of cling film. Using a rolling pin, bash each one to flatten it out to a thickness of about 1 cm (½ inch).
▸ Lay a slice of prosciutto over each flattened breast, top with the cheese, season and scatter with the sage. Fold the chicken breasts in half to completely encase the cheese and prosciutto.
▸ Place the flour on a large plate, the beaten eggs on another and the breadcrumbs on a third. Coat each chicken breast first in the flour, then the egg and finally the breadcrumbs.
▸ Heat the oil and butter in a large frying pan over a medium heat. When the foaming butter subsides, add the breadcrumbed chicken breasts and cook on both sides until lightly brown. Transfer to a roasting tin and cook in the oven for 10–15 minutes, until cooked through and golden brown.
▸ Two minutes before serving, make the sauce. Wipe the frying pan clean with kitchen paper and place on a medium-high heat. Add the butter and, when it starts to foam, add the sage, quickly followed by the lemon juice (take care as it may spit). Let it bubble for 15–20 seconds, then gently splash the sauce over the chicken breasts. Serve with buttered spring greens.

Tuna steak teriyaki style with Asian noodle-doodle salad

This is the type of Asian food that I return to again and again because it's fresh, fragrant, healthy and inviting. It's also stylish enough for a dinner party, and so easy to do that you have plenty of time to chat and drink with friends.

▸ Make the noodle-doodle salad first. Cook the noodles according to the packet instructions, then drain and refresh under cold running water. Make sure you shake off all the excess water, then place the noodles in a large bowl.

▸ Place the spring onions and chilli in a small bowl with the garlic, lime juice, sesame oil, fish sauce and sugar. Whisk together and pour over the noodles. Add the herbs and sesame seeds, mix until thoroughly combined and divide between four plates.

▸ Heat the oil and dried chilli in a large frying pan over a high heat. Add the tuna and cook quickly for about 40 seconds on each side (for steaks 2.5 cm/1 inch thick this timing will make them medium to medium-rare). Give them more or less time depending on the thickness of the tuna and how you like it cooked. Add the honey and soy sauce to the pan. Bubble furiously for 30 seconds, carefully turning the steaks two or three times in the sauce. (A pair of spring-loaded tongs makes light work of this.) Serve the tuna on top of the noodles, with the pan juices poured over and garnished with sprigs of coriander.

Serves 4
Preparation 10 mins
Cooking 5 mins
1 tablespoon sunflower oil
½ teaspoon crushed dried chilli
4 x 100–150-g (4–5-oz) tuna steaks
2 tablespoons clear honey
3 tablespoons soy sauce
sprigs fresh coriander, to serve

Noodle-doodle salad
150 g (5 oz) fine egg or rice noodles
6 spring onions, finely sliced
1 large, mild red chilli, seeded and
    finely chopped
2 garlic cloves, crushed
juice of 2 limes
2 tablespoons sesame oil
2 tablespoons fish sauce
pinch of sugar
3 tablespoons roughly chopped
    fresh coriander
2 tablespoons roughly fresh
    chopped mint
2 tablespoons toasted sesame seeds

Steak *au poivre* with rosemary rosti potatoes

Serves 2
Preparation 10 mins
Cooking 20 mins
400–500 g (14 oz – 1 lb 2 oz) waxy
   potatoes, such as Desirée
2 teaspoons finely chopped fresh
   rosemary leaves
2 tablespoons olive oil, plus extra
   for the steaks
50 g (2 oz) butter
2 sirloin steaks
2 shallots, finely chopped
2 tablespoons brandy
5 tablespoons crème fraîche
1 tablespoon green peppercorns
   in brine, rinsed
1 tablespoon Dijon mustard
salt and freshly ground black pepper

Good for recovering after a hard day's work

We all have difficult days. This scrumptious steak is sure to boost your energy levels and cheer you up. The splash of brandy should help you out, too!

Here's one of those dishes that's great for a cold winter or autumn night's dinner. I like to use soft green peppercorns in brine, which you can get in the spice section of most supermarkets and delis; they keep well in the fridge after opening. If you're using hard peppercorns, crush them coarsely with a pestle and mortar, or wrap them in a tea towel and bash them with a rolling pin, but don't use an electric mill as they will end up too fine and burn.

Squeezing out the excess moisture from the potatoes gives a much crisper rosti. The sauce in this dish also works well with fillet steak, chicken or pork.

▸ Peel and coarsely grate the potatoes into a tea towel, then gather the corners, twist to form a ball and squeeze out the excess water. Put the potatoes into a large bowl, add the rosemary and season well.
▸ Heat the oil and half the butter in a large frying pan over a medium heat. Divide the potatoes into four equal portions and add to the pan, flattening each portion slightly to make patties. Lower the heat a little and cook for about 5 minutes, until golden brown. Turn the rosti over and cook the other sides until golden and crisp. Remove from the pan and keep warm while you cook the steaks.
▸ Wipe any excess fat from the pan with kitchen paper and set the pan over a medium-high heat. Rub the steaks with a little oil, add seasoning and cook in the hot pan for 2–3 minutes on each side, depending on the thickness of the meat and how well cooked you like it. Remove from the pan and keep warm while you finish the sauce.
▸ Reduce the heat under the pan, melt the remaining butter, then add the shallots and cook for 30 seconds without colouring. Add the brandy and set it alight if you're feeling brave (don't panic – you're only burning off the alcohol, and the flames will die down in a few seconds). Stir in the crème fraîche and peppercorns and bring to the boil. Simmer for 30 seconds, then stir in the mustard and season well.
▸ Place two rosti on each of two warm plates and sit the steaks almost on top of them. Pour the peppercorn sauce over and serve immediately.

Sweet and sour pork Auntie G style

Auntie G was one of my mum's best friends from church, and being Chinese and a great cook, she made the best Chinese food ever. This was one of my favourite dinners, and her son Durk and I still make it to this day.

You could add a few handfuls of bean sprouts towards the end of cooking for extra crunch and texture.

▸ Trim the pork of any excess fat or sinew and cut into bite-size pieces. Heat the oil for deep frying in a wok or deep-fat fryer to 180°C/350°F.
▸ Meanwhile, prepare the batter. Whisk together the flour, 120 ml (4 fl oz) water, 1 tablespoon of the soy sauce and some seasoning. Add the pork pieces and mix to coat well. Using a slotted spoon or tongs, remove the pork pieces individually from the batter and carefully lower them into the hot oil. Deep-fry in batches for about 5 minutes, until golden and crisp. Drain on kitchen paper and keep warm.
▸ Now prepare the vegetables. Quarter and seed the peppers, then cut into chunks. Slice the spring onions into 2.5-cm (1-inch) lengths. Heat the tablespoon of oil in a large wok or sauté pan, add the peppers and spring onions and cook, stirring with a flat wooden spoon over a medium heat for about 2 minutes, until starting to soften. Add the bamboo shoots and pineapple chunks.
▸ Whisk all the sauce ingredients together add the remaining tablespoon of soy sauce and season. Pour over the vegetables and bring to the boil, then stir and simmer until thickened. Add the crisp fried pork and cook for a further 2–3 minutes. Serve with steamed jasmine rice and pak choi.

Serves 4
Preparation 25–30 mins
Cooking 20 mins
450 g (1 lb) pork tenderloin
500 ml (17 fl oz) sunflower oil,
    for deep frying
1 tablespoon sunflower oil,
    for stir frying
1 red pepper
1 green pepper
4 spring onions, trimmed
1 x 225-g (8-oz) can bamboo shoots,
    drained and rinsed
200 g (7 oz) tinned pineapple
    chunks, drained
salt and freshly ground black pepper

Batter
75 g (3 oz) plain flour
2 tablespoons soy sauce

Sauce
1 tablespoon cornflour
250 ml (8 fl oz) light chicken stock
    (Marigold Swiss chicken bouillon
    is good)
3 tablespoons soft light brown sugar
3 tablespoons rice vinegar or white
    wine vinegar
2 tablespoons tomato ketchup

Quick tip
Ingredients lists can look long, but a well-stocked store cupboard can help you prepare meals in minutes without cutting out the flavour.

Fresh and fabulous essentials

It's not necessary to overload with exotic and expensive ingredients, when a carefully chosen selection of store cupboard basics can feed you for weeks on end – here's a selection of simple, key items I couldn't live without.

Oils, vinegars and other bottled delights

My essentials oils are an all-purpose olive oil and extra-virgin olive oil (see page 11). You could also keep a good sesame oil for Asian cooking and perhaps a nut oil such as walnut for salad dressings. I recommend you keep bottles of good-quality vinegar to hand: red and white wine vinegar, and balsamic. The more expensive balsamic varieties are usually thick, syrupy and sometimes aged in oak barrels. Don't forget all your classic favourite sauces for spicing things up at a moment's notice: soy, fish, chilli, Worcester – whatever takes your fancy.

Sugar and spice and all things nice

I try to buy unrefined sugar – not only is this better for you, it also has a greater depth of flavour than white sugar which only adds sweetness and very little else. Sea salt is no lower in sodium than table salt, but it has a better flavour so less is needed. And don't forget the herbs and spices! These always tend to lurk at the back of the cupboard and go past their use-by date so buy in small quantities and re-stock regularly.

Pasta, pulses, rice and beans

Pasta is, of course, the definitive fast food! Keep at least one long thin variety for cream and tomato sauces and one shape such as rigatoni and shells for meaty sauces as they hold the sauce better. I always keep brown basmati rice and a good risotto to hand because their texture makes them a basis for many a great meal. And don't forget that pulses and beans are essential for high-fibre, high-protein and low-fat meals. Other grains to consider are cous cous, bulghar wheat and polenta, which feature a lot in the *Substantial salads* chapter of this book.

Knick-knacks

We all need the odd treat. Keep a selection of your favourite delicacies to smarten up even the most flung-together meal: capers, olives, sun-dried tomatoes, etc. A quality tin of tomatoes or purée can transform a pasta sauce or casserole, and tinned fish such as sardines and anchovies are especially good for jazzing up pizzas. There's so much to choose from, your store cupboard will be packed with feel-goodness.

Flamme tart

This is a light and quick alternative to a quiche. Although ideal for supper, this tart is so easy to prepare that it could also be cut into small squares and served as a nibble with drinks.

▸ Preheat the oven to 200°C/400°F/Gas mark 6 and place a large, heavy baking sheet on the middle shelf.
▸ Heat the oil in a large frying pan over a medium heat, add the pancetta and cook for a couple of minutes, until the fat starts to run and become translucent.
▸ Add the onions to the pan and continue to cook for a further 10 minutes, stirring occasionally until they and the pancetta begin to turn golden. Add the garlic and thyme and cook for a further 30 seconds. Season well.
▸ While the onions are cooking, unroll the pastry on to another large baking sheet and score a line about 2.5 cm (1 inch) in from the edges to create a frame. Prick all over so that it doesn't rise too high. Put the baking sheet into the oven on top of the hot baking sheet already in the oven and cook the pastry for about 7 minutes, until very lightly golden.
▸ Season the crème fraîche and spread half of it over the pastry, taking care not to cover the outer frame. Arrange the onions and pancetta on top. Dot over the remaining crème fraîche, then return the sheet to the oven for a further 20–25 minutes, until the pastry is golden and the filling is bubbling. Serve warm with a crisp green salad dressed with a mustardy vinaigrette.

Serves 4–6
Preparation 10 mins
Cooking 35 mins
1 tablespoon olive oil
150 g (5 oz) diced pancetta
3 medium onions, sliced
1 fat garlic clove, crushed
1 teaspoon fresh thyme leaves
375 g (13 oz) ready-rolled puff pastry
250 g (9 oz) crème fraîche
salt and freshly ground black pepper

Tagliatelle with lemon chicken, ricotta and herbs

If you want to knock up something impressive with the least amount of effort, this tasty dish has to be for you. It's one of my midweek saviours. Use ready-cooked chicken breasts for this super supper dish.

Egg tagliatelle generally takes less time to cook than other types of pasta, and their lighter texture works well with the ingredients in this recipe. My son likes to mix some crispy bacon pieces into his serving, whilst the missus likes toasted pine nuts.

▸ Bring a large pan of salted water to the boil for the tagliatelle and cook according to the packet instructions.
▸ While the pasta is cooking, cut or shred the chicken breasts into bite-size pieces.
▸ Drain the pasta through a colander, reserving a cupful of the cooking water. Tip the pasta back into the pan, add the ricotta, butter, chicken and half the reserved cooking water. Stir to melt the ricotta into the pasta, adding a little more water if it looks dry.
▸ Stir in the rocket, parsley and lemon zest. Season well and add the nutmeg. Add a squeeze of lemon juice and serve immediately with freshly grated Parmesan to hand around.

Serves 4
Preparation 5 mins
Cooking 15 mins
350–400 g (12–14 oz) tagliatelle
2 cooked chicken breasts
grated zest and juice of 1 unwaxed lemon
250 g (9 oz) ricotta
25 g (1 oz) butter
handful of wild rocket
2 tablespoons roughly chopped fresh flatleaf parsley
pinch of freshly grated nutmeg
freshly grated Parmesan, to serve
salt and freshly ground black pepper

Roasted Parma-wrapped halibut with sage lentils

Serves 4
Preparation 5 mins
Cooking 30 mins

1 carrot
1 stick celery
1 onion
2 tablespoons olive oil
1 garlic clove, crushed
6 fresh sage leaves, chopped
½ teaspoon English mustard
1 x 200-g (7-oz) can chopped
   tomatoes
1 x 410-g (14½-oz) can lentils, drained
150 ml (¼ pint) vegetable stock
pinch sugar
4 slices Parma ham or similar
4 x 150–175-g (5–6-oz) halibut fillets
1–2 tablespoons chopped fresh
   parsley
salt and freshly ground black pepper

Good for giving in to temptation

The title of this dish sounds succulent and the colours are simply alluring. Give in and enjoy this fabulous meal of irresistible, yet wholesome, ingredients.

I love dishes where you can just wrap things up and pop them in the oven while you make a simple accompaniment. This recipe fits the bill and makes a very stylish meal in minutes. You could use salmon or haddock instead of halibut.

▸ Preheat the oven to 220°C/425°F/Gas mark 7 and place a baking sheet on the top shelf.
▸ Chop the carrot and celery into small dice and finely chop the onion. Alternatively, cut the carrot and celery into large pieces, and blitz them in a food processor for 5 seconds, then quarter the onion, add it to the other vegetables and blitz again for another 5 seconds.
▸ Heat 1 tablespoon of the oil in a sauté pan, add the vegetables and cook over a medium heat for 5 minutes. Add the garlic and sage and continue to cook for a further couple of minutes. Stir in the mustard, tomatoes, lentils, stock, sugar and the rest of the oil and season well. Bring to the boil, reduce the heat and simmer gently for about 7 minutes.
▸ Wrap a slice of Parma ham around each halibut fillet, and place on the hot baking sheet. Roast for about 10 minutes, until the fish is cooked through.
▸ Stir the parsley into the lentils, check the seasoning, and divide the lentils between four warm plates. Top with the Parma-wrapped halibut fillets and serve.

Midweek meals

Salmon and spinach fishcakes with beetroot and horseradish relish

Serves 4
Preparation 25 mins
Cooking 15 mins
450 g (1 lb) skinless, boneless
  salmon fillet
2 tablespoons olive oil
450 g (1 lb) floury potatoes
1 x 175-g (6-oz) bag young leaf
  spinach, washed
grated zest of ½ unwaxed lemon
1 tablespoon capers, rinsed and
  finely chopped
2–3 tablespoons plain flour
25 g (1 oz) butter
salt and freshly ground black pepper
watercress, salad and lemon wedges
  to serve

Beetroot and horseradish relish
250 g (9 oz) beetroot
1 heaped teaspoon horseradish
  sauce
1 tablespoon chopped fresh parsley
1 tablespoon snipped fresh chives
2 heaped tablespoons low-fat Greek
  yoghurt or half-fat crème fraîche
2–3 teaspoons lemon juice

These fishcakes can be made in advance and freeze well. Use fresh beetroot if in season – roast or boil them leaving at least 5 mm (½ inch) of stalk at the top because, if too closely trimmed, they will 'bleed', losing colour and some of their flavour. Incidentally, the leaves are edible and can be used in salads. If you use pre-cooked beetroot, avoid ones that have been dipped in vinegar. You could also use fresh horseradish if available instead of the ready-made sauce.

▶ Preheat the oven to 190°C/375°F/Gas mark 5.
▶ Drizzle the salmon with 2 teaspoons of the oil, season, cover with foil and bake in the oven for 15–20 minutes, until cooked through. Cool, then flake the fish into pieces. You could use a fork to do this.
▶ Meanwhile, peel and quarter the potatoes. Cook in boiling salted water for 15 minutes, or until tender. Drain thoroughly, cool slightly and mash until smooth.
▶ Pop the spinach into a sauté pan, add 2 tablespoons water, then cover and cook for 2–3 minutes, until wilted. Alternatively, cook in the bag in the microwave according to the packet instructions. Drain well, cool and roughly chop.
▶ In a large bowl mix together the mashed potato, flaked salmon and chopped spinach. Add the lemon zest and capers, season well and mix until combined. Divide the mixture into eight equal portions and shape into patties. Cover and chill while you prepare the relish.
▶ Coarsely grate the beetroot, and add the horseradish, parsley, chives and yoghurt or crème fraîche . Season well, mix to combine, then taste and add lemon juice as required.
▶ Lightly coat the fishcakes in the flour. Heat half the butter and 1 tablespoon of the oil in a large frying pan. Add four of the fishcakes and cook for about 8 minutes, until golden brown, turning them over halfway through. Remove from the pan and keep warm while you cook the remaining fishcakes, adding the remaining butter and more oil to the pan if needed. Serve immediately with a watercress salad, lemon wedges and the beetroot and horseradish relish.

Dreamy pancetta and dolcelatte risotto

This recipe definitely falls into the comfort food category – it's so wonderfully indulgent. Pancetta is smoked bacon, and it's best to buy it in one piece from a deli because it has a better flavour than pre-sliced stuff. It's easy to slice and keeps well in the fridge.

▸ Heat the oil in a sauté pan, add the pancetta and cook until the fat begins to run and the pancetta starts to brown. Add the shallots or onion and cook until translucent. Stir in the garlic and sage and cook for 30 seconds. Heat the stock in another saucepan.

▸ Tip the rice into the sauté pan and cook, stirring continuously, for 1 minute.

▸ Pour in the white wine whilst continuing to stir, but be careful as it might bubble up and spit. Continue to stir over a medium heat until almost all the liquid has been absorbed. Lower the heat slightly and add the hot stock one ladleful at a time, stirring after each addition. Wait until each ladleful has been almost absorbed before adding more stock. Continue until almost all the stock has been added to the rice: this will take about 15–20 minutes.

▸ Taste the rice: it should be slightly *al dente*. Remove from the heat and stir in the butter and half the Parmesan. Season with pepper – the risotto may not need salt as the Parmesan and pancetta are both quite salty.

▸ Divide the risotto between four warm bowls, crumble the dolcelatte over the top and serve immediately with the remaining Parmesan.

Quick tip

For a sexy dinner party you could add porcini mushrooms to this recipe – available dried – or fresh asparagus.

Serves 4
Preparation 5 mins
Cooking 25–30 mins
1 tablespoon olive oil
150 g (5 oz) diced pancetta
4 shallots or 1 onion, finely chopped
2 garlic cloves, crushed
1 tablespoon finely chopped
   fresh sage
approx. 1.5 litres (2½ pints) light
   chicken or vegetable stock
350 g (12 oz) arborio rice
200 ml (7 fl oz) dry white wine
25 g (1 oz) butter
100g (4 oz) freshly grated Parmesan
100 g (4 oz) dolcelatte cheese
freshly ground black pepper

Egg, potato and herb tortilla with grilled sausages and fresh tomato salsa

Serves 4
Preparation 15 mins
Cooking 20 mins
500g (1 lb 2 oz) floury potatoes
8 good-quality sausages
1 onion, sliced
1 garlic clove, crushed
2 tablespoons olive oil
25 g (1 oz) butter
2 tablespoons snipped fresh chives
1 tablespoon chopped fresh parsley
1 teaspoon chopped fresh thyme
   leaves
6 large eggs, beaten
salt and freshly ground black pepper

Salsa
4 plum tomatoes
1 small red onion
1 green chilli (optional)
pinch of cayenne
1 tablespoon chopped fresh parsley

I like my tortilla to have a bit of a kick, but feel free to leave out the chilli. This type of slow-cook omelette is easy to serve, and any leftovers can be packed into a lunch box or served with salad.

▸ Peel the potatoes, cut them into 2-cm (³/4-inch) chunks and cook in boiling salted water until just tender. Drain and cool slightly.
▸ Preheat the grill and cook the sausages on a foil-lined baking tray. Keep warm.
▸ Meanwhile, make the salsa. Finely dice the tomatoes, onion and chilli (if using). Add the cayenne, parsley and a pinch of a salt and set aside.
▸ Heat the oil and butter over a medium heat in a 20-cm (8-inch) non-stick frying pan, add the onion and cook until just beginning to turn golden at the edges. Add the garlic and cook for a further 30 seconds. Add the drained potatoes, season, reduce the heat slightly and cook for 5 minutes, until the potatoes are tender and lightly golden. Sprinkle in the herbs.
▸ Pour the eggs into the pan, allowing them to run around and between the potatoes (a wooden spatula will help you do this). Cook over a low heat until the eggs are almost set. Slide the pan under the grill and cook until the top of the omelette is golden brown. Serve cut into wedges with the sausages and the tomato salsa.

Quick tip
Break the eggs into a separate bowl first before adding to the pan to avoid broken bits of shell ruining the whole recipe.

Parmesan-crusted cheese and ham macaroni

Serves 4
Preparation 5 mins
Cooking 40 mins
75 g (3 oz) butter
50 g (2 oz) plain flour
600 ml (1 pint) semi-skimmed milk
1 bay leaf
225 g (8 oz) mascarpone
1 tablespoon Dijon mustard
225 g (8 oz) mature Cheddar, grated
400 g (14 oz) rigatoni pasta
125 g (5 oz) lean ham, diced
2 tablespoons chopped fresh parsley
1 tablespoon fresh breadcrumbs
1 tablespoon freshly grated
  Parmesan
salt and freshly ground black pepper

Good for late-night snacking
This savoury dish can be prepared in advance and really hits the spot when hunger calls.

For this absolute classic, which you can prepare in advance, you could use pancetta or bacon instead of ham: just sauté in a pan for a few minutes before adding to the pasta. The mascarpone makes the sauce extra-creamy and indulgent.

▸ Melt the butter in a saucepan. Add the flour and cook for 1 minute, stirring constantly. Slowly pour in the milk, whisking all the time. Add the bay leaf and bring to the boil. Reduce the heat and simmer very gently for about 5 minutes, until smooth and thickened, stirring occasionally. Remove from the heat, remove the bay leaf and add the mascarpone, mustard and Cheddar. Mix until smooth, then season. Cover the surface of the sauce with cling film to prevent a skin forming.
▸ Preheat the oven to 200°C/400°F/Gas mark 6.
▸ Bring a large pan of salted water to the boil. Add the rigatoni, stir to separate and cook for 1 minute less than the time suggested on the packet. Drain thoroughly and return to the pan.
▸ Pour the cheese sauce over the cooked rigatoni and add the ham and parsley. Mix thoroughly and tip into an ovenproof gratin dish. Combine the breadcrumbs and Parmesan and scatter over the rigatoni. Bake on the middle shelf of the oven for about 20 minutes, until the top is golden brown and bubbling. Serve with a crisp green salad and a crusty baguette.

Grilled trout fillets with saffron and tomato rice

You can't beat fresh fish: it's wonderfully nutritious and, as my fishmonger says, 'The quicker a fresh fish is on the fire after it's caught, the better it is'. Trout is one of those fish that really suffers from overcooking; it tastes far better if eaten slightly underdone than overdone. The time I have set should cook it perfectly. Your fishmonger will fillet the trout for you.

▸ Place the rice in a bowl, cover with cold water and leave to soak for 10 minutes. Crumble the saffron threads into a small bowl, add 2 tablespoons boiling water and infuse for 10 minutes.

▸ Melt the butter in a large sauté pan, add the onion and garlic and cook over a low to medium heat for about 3–4 minutes, until tender and starting to turn golden at the edges. Drain the rice and add to the pan with the saffron infusion and bay leaf. Mix well to coat in the buttery onions, add the stock and bring to the boil. Reduce the heat to a very gentle simmer, then cover and cook for 10 minutes, until almost all the stock has been absorbed.

▸ Preheat the grill. Meanwhile, cut the fresh tomatoes in half, scoop out and discard the seeds, and roughly chop the flesh. Slice the sun-dried tomatoes into slivers. Add all the tomatoes to the rice, stir to combine and remove the pan from the heat. Leave the pan covered while you cook the fish.

▸ Lay the trout fillets, skin-side down, on a foil-lined baking sheet, rub with a little olive oil, then season and place under the grill for 3–4 minutes, until cooked through. Stir the parsley into the rice and serve immediately with the trout fillets. Drizzle with a little extra-virgin olive oil, add a twist of pepper and garnish with sprigs of parsley.

Serves 4
Preparation 15 mins
Cooking 20 mins
250 g (9 oz) basmati rice
large pinch of saffron threads
25 g (1 oz) butter
1 large onion, sliced
1 garlic clove, crushed
1 bay leaf
600 ml (1 pint) vegetable or light chicken stock
3 large ripe tomatoes
6 sun-dried tomatoes
8 medium-sized fresh trout fillets
2 tablespoons chopped fresh parsley, plus sprigs to garnish
salt and freshly ground black pepper

Soy-poached chicken breasts with pak choi, coconut rice and hot and sour sauce

People sometimes say they prefer a nice juicy thigh or leg of chicken because they find the breast too dry. That's often because it's been overcooked. Poaching helps to avoid this, and it's also a healthy way of cooking, but don't overdo it: the chicken should be lovely and moist, not falling to bits.

If you're short of time, you can use a ready-made oyster sauce instead of making the hot and sour sauce.

▸ Place the rice in a bowl, cover with cold water and soak for 15–20 minutes. Drain and rinse. Tip into a saucepan, add the coconut milk, 300 ml (½ pint) water and the salt. Bring to the boil and reduce the heat to a very gentle simmer. Cover and cook for 10 minutes, until the rice is tender.

▸ While the rice is cooking, shred the lime leaves and place in a saucepan. Peel and slice the ginger and garlic and roughly chop the chilli. Add to the pan with the soy sauce and 600 ml (1 pint) water. Bring to the boil, add the chicken breasts, then cover and cook over a low heat for 4 minutes. Turn the chicken in the liquid and simmer for a further 2 minutes, or until cooked through.

▸ Meanwhile, trim the pak choi, cut them in half through the root and cook in a steamer set over the chicken pan for 3 minutes, or until tender.

▸ Make the sauce while the pak choi is steaming. Whisk all the ingredients together in a small saucepan, place over a medium heat and bring to the boil. Simmer for 1 minute, stirring constantly until thickened and glossy.

▸ Arrange the slices on plates or in bowls with the coconut rice and pak choi. Drizzle with the sauce, scatter with the spring onions and sesame seeds, and serve immediately.

Serves 4
Preparation 20 mins
Cooking 15 mins
225 g (8 oz) basmati rice
150 ml (¼ pint) coconut milk
2 lime leaves, fresh or dried
2-cm (1-inch) piece fresh ginger
1 garlic clove
½ large red chilli, seeded
1 tablespoon light soy sauce
4 skinless chicken breasts
4 heads pak choi
4 spring onions, chopped
1 tablespoon toasted sesame seeds
pinch of salt

Hot and sour sauce
4 tablespoons caster sugar
1 heaped teaspoon cornflour
4 tablespoons rice vinegar
4 tablespoons light soy sauce
2 tablespoons rice wine or dry sherry

Good for your stomach
There are a lot of flavours in this dish, but poaching is a lighter method of cooking than roasting and the delicate, fragrant ingredients make this recipe easy to digest.

Crisp salmon fillets with braised red peppers

Serves 4
Preparation 10 mins
Cooking 45 mins
4 red peppers, quartered and seeded
2 garlic cloves
6 tablespoons fruity olive oil
2 medium-sized red onions, sliced
120 ml (4 fl oz) passata
2 anchovy fillets in olive oil
2 tablespoons roughly chopped
    fresh basil
4 x 150-g (5-oz) salmon fillets with
    skin on
salt and freshly ground black pepper

**Good for your
concentration levels**
New research suggests that
oily fish can improve your
concentration levels –
especially good news for
getting your kids to stay
focused!

Salmon has a rich flavour, so the sweetness of the peppers is a good contrast. This recipe can also be made with haddock, cod or sea bass fillets, and you can leave out the anchovies if you wish – but that would be shame, as they cook down and are used just for seasoning the dish. A small can of chopped tomatoes can be used in place of passata: both are good store-cupboard items.

▸ Cut the peppers into 1-cm (½-inch) strips. Lightly smash each garlic clove with the flat side of a knife. Heat 4 tablespoons of the oil in a large sauté pan. Add the peppers, onions and garlic, season and cook over a low to medium heat for about 10 minutes, until the peppers start to soften.
▸ Add the passata and anchovies to the pan. Cover, reduce the heat and cook gently for about 30 minutes, until the peppers and onions are meltingly tender. Remove the garlic from the pan, add the basil and check the seasoning.
▸ Slash the skin of each salmon fillet four or five times, and season all over. Heat the remaining two tablespoons of oil in a large frying pan, add the salmon fillets skin-side down and cook for about 3 minutes, until the skin is crisp and browned. Turn the fillets over and cook for a further 2 minutes, until cooked through. Serve the salmon with the peppers and steamed and buttered spring greens or spinach.

Beef Stroganof with buttered tagliatelle

Serves 4
Preparation 5 mins
Cooking 20 mins
350–400 g (12–14 oz) tagliatelle
650 g (1 lb 6 oz) rump or fillet
    tail steak
50 g (2 oz) butter
2 tablespoons olive oil, for frying
1 large onion, sliced
250 g (9 oz) chestnut mushrooms,
    thickly sliced
1–2 teaspoons paprika
2 tablespoons brandy (optional)
300 ml (½ pint) sour cream
    or crème fraîche
1 tablespoon lemon juice
1 tablespoon chopped parsley
salt and freshly ground black pepper

They say bistro-style food is coming back into fashion, so that means Stroganof and coq au vin will soon be all the rage again.

This classic Russian dish is quick to prepare, so is ideal for a supper party when time is short. Ask your butcher for fillet tail: not only is it cheaper, but you don't feel so guilty about slicing it up.

▸ Bring a large pan of salted water to the boil for the tagliatelle.
▸ Meanwhile, trim any excess fat from the steak and cut the meat into strips no thicker than your little finger.
▸ Heat half the butter and 1 tablespoon of the oil in a large sauté pan. Add the onion and cook over a medium heat for 2–3 minutes, until beginning to soften. Add the mushrooms to the pan and cook until tender. Add the paprika and cook for a further 30 seconds. Tip the onion and mushrooms on to a plate and set aside.
▸ Cook the tagliatelle according to the packet instructions, then drain and toss in the remaining butter.
▸ While the pasta is cooking, finish the Stroganof. Place the sauté pan over a really high heat and add 1 tablespoon of the remaining oil. Season the steak strips and add half to the hot pan, cooking very quickly until browned all over. Remove from the pan using a slotted spoon and transfer to the same plate as the onion and mushrooms. Cook the remaining steak in the hot pan, adding extra oil if needed.
▸ Return the mushrooms, onions, steak and all the juices to the pan. Add the brandy (if using) and the sour cream or crème fraîche, bring to the boil and simmer for 1–2 minutes, until slightly thickened. Season well and add the lemon juice. Scatter with the parsley and serve immediately with the buttered tagliatelle.

Quick tip
If you don't have sour cream to hand, use double cream and add a touch of lemon juice.

Cajun-style tofu and butternut squash with watercress and avocado salad

Tofu is packed full of protein and vitamins. It's brilliant for soaking up other flavours and is the perfect healthy substitute for meat, fish or chicken.

▸ Place the fennel, cumin and coriander seeds in a small frying pan. Add the crushed dried chilli and place over a low to medium heat for about 1 minute until the spices start to release their aromas. Tip into a pestle, add the oregano, garlic powder and paprika and pound with the mortar until finely ground.

▸ Preheat the oven to 220°C/430°F/Gas mark 7.

▸ Peel and de-seed the butternut squash and cut the flesh into chunks. Place in a bowl, add 1 tablespoon of oil and 2 teaspoons of the spice blend. Mix to thoroughly coat the butternut squash in the mixture, tip into a roasting tin and then roast on the middle shelf of the oven for 20 minutes.

▸ Drain the tofu and pat dry on kitchen paper. Cut into 2-cm (1-inch) cubes and place in a bowl with the onion. Toss in a little oil and 1 heaped teaspoon of the spice blend. Add to the butternut squash and cook for a further 20 minutes until golden brown.

▸ Meanwhile prepare the salad. Peel and stone the avocado and cut the flesh into slices. Combine the soy sauce, remaining oil, sugar, ginger and crushed garlic in a small bowl. Season and whisk until smooth.

▸ Arrange a handful or watercress on four plates, add some avocado pieces and drizzle with the dressing. Divide the spiced butternut squash, tofu and red onion over the top and serve immediately.

Serves 4
Preparation 15 mins
Cooking 40 mins
1 teaspoon fennel seeds
2 teaspoons cumin seeds
2 teaspoons coriander seeds
1 teaspoon crushed dried chillies
1 teaspoon dried oregano or thyme
½ teaspoon garlic powder
½ teaspoon paprika
1 butternut squash
5 tablespoons fruity olive oil
250 g tofu
1 red onion, peeled and thickly sliced

Salad
1 ripe avocado
1 tablespoon soy sauce
pinch of soft light brown sugar
1 teaspoon grated fresh ginger
1 small clove garlic, crushed
75 g (3 oz) watercress
salt and freshly ground black pepper

Fabulous feast: Mediterranean

If you like hosting big family dos, then you'll be used to people turning up at all times of the day expecting to be fed. A Mediterranean theme is a great way of breaking free from stale buffets and providing a fresh, day-long feast. The idea is to steer away from strict breakfast, lunch and dinner times, taking the time to relax, laugh, socialise – and, of course, eat glorious food.

Mediterranean food is diverse and inspiring. Many dishes include the fresh catch of the day and pick of the garden, so you're sure to get a range of flavours. Try a mid- to late-morning breakfast with plenty of sweet treats that you can prepare beforehand and will fill everyone up. Lunch should be the biggest meal of the day, adopting the proper Italian style of antipasti, plenty of pasta options and several main course options. It's hard work and certainly not a light affair, but the full meal spread will last for hours – leaving the evening free for you to relax.

Menu ideas

Late-morning breakfast

Spinach, Cheddar and Parmesan muffins with a cream cheese centre **page 30**
Fluffy smoked salmon omelette **page 17**

The lunch feast

Antipasti
Bruschetta with tomatoes, roasted peppers and marinated anchovies **page 55**
Fennel, pear and Parma ham salad **page 72**

Primo piatti
Penne with roasted cherry tomato and melting taleggio sauce **page 88**
Spaghetti with Sicilain cauliflower sauce **page 95**
Dreamy pancetta and dolcelatte risotto **page 117**

Secondo piatti
Roasted Parma-wrapped halibut with sage lentils **page 110**
Flamme tart **page 109**

Dolci
Poached peaches with vanilla and sweet Muscat wine **page 146**
Frozen strawberry yoghurt **page 155**

Lamb meatballs in tomato sauce with couscous

Serves 4
Preparation 15 mins
Cooking 40 mins
4 medium slices white bread,
  crusts removed
milk, for soaking
1 onion, roughly chopped
2 garlic cloves, roughly chopped
1 tablespoon ground cumin
1 teaspoon ground coriander
500 g (1 lb 2 oz) lamb mince
2 tablespoons chopped fresh
  coriander
grated zest of ½ unwaxed lemon
1 medium egg, beaten
1 tablespoon olive oil, for frying
salt and freshly ground black pepper

Tomato sauce
1 tablespoon olive oil
1 onion, finely chopped
1 garlic clove, finely chopped
1 x 680-g (1 lb 7-oz) jar passata
1 small cinnamon stick
1 teaspoon caster sugar
2 bay leaves

Casablanca couscous
250 g (9 oz) couscous
juice of ½ lemon
2 tablespoons extra-virgin olive oil
50 g (2 oz) raisins
50 g (2 oz) toasted pine nuts
1 tablespoon chopped fresh
  flatleaf parsley

This is one of my family's all-time favourite dishes, and is even a hit with some of my daughter's friends who are awkward eaters – although I have to serve it with rice instead of couscous. You can spice up the meatballs for adults with a little cayenne and serve with Greek yoghurt to which a tablespoon of toasted cumin seeds have been added.

▸ Soak the bread in milk and gently squeeze out until dry. Whiz the onion and garlic in a food processor with the cumin and ground coriander. Add the lamb, fresh coriander, lemon zest, bread and beaten egg and season with salt and plenty of pepper. Process again until well combined.

▸ Using wet hands, roll the lamb mixture into 24 walnut-sized balls; cover and set aside.

▸ Make the sauce. Heat the oil in an oven-proof sauté pan over a medium heat, add the onion and garlic and cook until just beginning to turn golden at the edges. Add the passata, cinnamon, sugar and bay leaves and season. Bring to the boil, reduce the heat and simmer gently for 10 minutes.

▸ Preheat the oven to 200°C/400°F/Gas mark 6.

▸ Heat 1 tablespoon olive oil in a large frying pan and add half the meatballs. Fry over a medium-high heat until brown all over. Remove from the pan with a slotted spoon and fry the remaining meatballs, adding more oil if needed.

▸ Add all the meatballs to the tomato sauce and place on the middle shelf of the oven for 20–25 minutes while you prepare the couscous.

▸ Bring 400 ml (14 fl oz) salted water to the boil in a medium saucepan. Add the couscous and stir well, then cover with a lid, remove from the heat and leave for 5 minutes. Fluff the couscous with a fork, then add the lemon juice, oil, raisins and pine nuts. Season, scatter with the parsley and serve immediately with the meatballs in tomato sauce.

Whole sea bass baked Thai style

Sea bass, whether striped, black or silver, has a delicately flavoured, creamy flesh that works really well with strong flavours. In this recipe the fish is steamed in a foil bag, which, when opened, fills the air with beautiful Thai aromas.

Take care when you chop chillies, or there can be dire consequences. My mum used to rub a little oil into her hands before she chopped chilli, and washed them immediately afterwards to remove the heat. I always do the same so that I don't have any emergencies in the men's room!

▸ Preheat the oven to 190°C/375°F/Gas mark 5.
▸ Cut the ginger into matchsticks. Finely chop the chilli. Chop the spring onions. Place these ingredients in a bowl with the garlic. Add the sugar, soy sauce, fish sauce, coriander and lime juice, and mix well.
▸ Wash the fish and pat dry with kitchen paper. Using a sharp knife, carefully make four or five diagonal slashes on both sides of each fish. Cut two large pieces of foil and place one fish in the middle of each piece. Pull the sides of the foil up slightly to prevent any leakage.
▸ Spoon some of the soy and ginger mixture into the cavity of each fish and drizzle the rest over the top. Wrap tightly in the foil, place on a baking sheet and cook on the middle shelf of the oven for 25–30 minutes, until the fish is cooked through.
▸ Open the foil bags at the dining table so that everyone can enjoy the aromatic moment. Sprinkle with coriander and serve immediately with steamed jasmine rice and Pak choi with honey, soy and sesame seeds (page 177).

Quick tip
Ask your fishmonger to gut and scale the fish for you – it's so much easier than doing it yourself.

Serves 4
Preparation 10 mins
Cooking 25–30 mins
1 x 5-cm (2-inch) piece fresh ginger, peeled
1 large red chilli, seeded
4 spring onions, trimmed
2 garlic cloves, crushed
2 teaspoons caster sugar
4 tablespoons soy sauce
2 tablespoons fish sauce
3 tablespoons chopped fresh coriander, plus a handful for sprinkling
juice of 2 limes
2 x 750-g (1¾-lb) sea bass, gutted and scaled

Mussels in cider and crème fraîche with salt-crusted home-made oven chips

Serves 2
Preparation 10 mins
Cooking 40 mins
750 g (1½ lb) waxy potatoes
2 tablespoons sunflower or
    groundnut oil
flaky sea salt, for the chips
1 kg (2¼ lb) live mussels
1 leek, washed
2 shallots
25 g (1 oz) butter
1 garlic clove, crushed
250 ml (8 fl oz) dry cider
4 tablespoons crème fraîche
2 tablespoons roughly chopped
    fresh parsley
salt and freshly ground black pepper

Mussels use to be referred to as the 'poor man's shellfish', just as monkfish was the 'poor man's scampi'. How times have changed! Now some restaurants build whole menus around these ingredients.

Green-lipped mussels from New Zealand are larger, meatier and have a more distinctive flavour than their European counterparts. Once they have opened, I like to sprinkle them with herby garlic-butter breadcrumbs and flash them under the grill. When buying the inexpensive blue-black variety, go for medium to small mussels, as large ones are not so appetizing. Always buy more than you need to allow for the odd dodgy mussel you have to throw away.

▸ Preheat the oven to 220°C/425°F/Gas mark 7.
▸ Wash the potatoes and cook them whole in boiling water for 10 minutes. Drain and, when cool enough to handle, cut into chunky chips. Place in a bowl with the oil and mix to coat thoroughly. Arrange the chips in a single layer on a large baking sheet, season with sea salt and bake for about 35–40 minutes, until golden brown and crisp.
▸ When the chips have been cooking for about 20 minutes, start to prepare the mussels. Fill a clean sink with cold water and tip in the mussels. Check each one and discard any with cracked or chipped shells. Give any open mussels a sharp tap: if they do not close up tightly, discard them too. If the mussels have a fibrous beard attached, pull it out and off with your fingers. Rinse off any grit or dirt and place the mussels in a bowl of clean, cold water until you are ready to cook them.
▸ Thinly slice the leek and shallots: you can use the slicing blade on your food processor if you like. Melt the butter in a pan that's large enough to hold all the mussels and has a tight-fitting lid. Add the leek and shallots and cook over a medium heat for about 3 minutes, until starting to soften. Add the garlic and cook for a further 30 seconds.
▸ Drain the mussels and tip them into the pan, then add the cider and bring to the boil. Cover with the lid and cook for 3–5 minutes, giving the pan an occasional shake, until all the mussels are wide open.
▸ Using a slotted spoon, scoop the mussels into a large serving bowl and cover with a cloth or piece of foil to keep warm. Return the pan to the heat and reduce the cider by half. Add the crème fraîche and boil for 30 seconds. Check the seasoning, then pour the liquor over the mussels. Scatter with the parsley and serve immediately with the oven chips (sprinkled with a little sea salt) and plenty of napkins.

Fresh and fabulous atmosphere

Getting people together and eating some wonderful food is probably one of my favourite pastimes. I know I'm a chef, but the beauty of that is that I can share recipes with you that are approachable, friendly and leave lots of time for you to mingle with your guests instead of being stressed and constantly under pressure. The trick is not to overload, giving yourself the additional headache of cooking three complicated dishes. It means that you, the host, are not chained to the stove while your guests are left to themselves with the wine!

Clever planning; smooth running

If using the cooker for the main course then serve either something cold or a dish that can be cooked on the stove top for the starter. Try to serve one course that can be prepared in advance; casseroles are perfect, requiring only reheating.

Think thirst first

When people first arrive, you don't want to be running around organizing drinks so why not have a tray of cocktails at the ready? Try fresh and fruity ingredients in summer or simple champagne cocktails when you're really splashing out.

Get your records on

I think music is one of the most important aspects of creating a feel-good atmosphere, but there's nothing more annoying than having to break in the middle of a dinner party and go off to sort through your CDs. Select music in advance, choosing songs that make you happy and relaxed – your guests will pick up on your mood and follow suit.

Natural presentation

Sometimes all you need are natural candles and fresh flowers to decorate the feel-good atmosphere – if it's summer why not lay a table in the garden and hang some night lights in the trees. Try not to put on a complicated spread of dinnerware – you could just bring out the good old china!

Nothing wrong with a little help here and there!

Why not serve something shop-bought for either the starter or dessert? French patisseries make excellent fruit tarts; simply add some good quality ice cream and everyone's happy. A fabulous selection of cheese and biscuits is easy to prepare and impressive to look at. Follow this with some decadent chocolates and a pot of freshly made coffee.

Linguine with fresh crab, asparagus, lemon and basil

Serves 4
Preparation 5 mins
Cooking 20 mins
350 g (12 oz) linguine
250 g (9 oz) asparagus
3 tablespoons extra-virgin olive oil
1 garlic clove, crushed
pinch of chilli flakes or cayenne
125 ml (4 fl oz) double cream
250 g (9 oz) fresh white crabmeat
2 tablespoons chopped fresh basil
grated zest of 1 unwaxed lemon

Good for a taste of holiday
The taste of fresh shellfish tends to evoke our fondest holiday memories. It's worth remembering that Britain has plenty of places to source quality fresh fish so you can feel like you're on holiday any time of the year.

Crab's a wonderful thing at the seaside, and it can taste almost as good at home, especially when it's combined with new-season asparagus or fresh podded peas. Fresh crab meat is best, but if it isn't available, use tinned.

▸ Bring a large pan of salted water to the boil, add the linguine, stir to prevent them sticking and cook according to the packet instructions. Drain well.
▸ Meanwhile, trim the asparagus and cut into 2.5-cm (1-inch) lengths. Cook in boiling salted water for about 3 minutes, until tender, then drain. Heat the oil in another large pan. Add the garlic and chilli or cayenne and cook for 30 seconds. Add the cream, asparagus and crabmeat and heat gently.
▸ Tip the linguine into the cream mixture and toss gently over a low heat to combine. Divide between four warm bowls, scatter with the basil and lemon zest and serve immediately.

Caribbean bouillabaisse
with chilli rouille

Fish, fish, ooh beautiful fish! I've included clams and mussels, but see what shellfish look best at the fishmonger's on the day. If you don't have all the listed spices in your larder, a tablespoon of curry powder will suffice, but saffron is a must (remember that a little goes a long way).

You can use either sweet potatoes or Charlottes, or a mixture of both. Yum!

▸ Make the rouille first. Soak the saffron in 1–2 tablespoon hot water for 5 minutes.

▸ Place the egg yolks in a bowl, add the mustard and garlic and mix with a balloon whisk for a couple of minutes, until the mixture starts to turn pale. Add the oil a few drops at a time, whisking constantly until each addition is thoroughly incorporated before adding the next. Continue in this way until about two-thirds of the oil has been added and the rouille has started to thicken. Add the remaining oil in a thin stream, whisking all the time. Add the saffron and 1 teaspoon of its soaking liquid and the harissa, lemon juice and some seasoning. Cover and chill until required. (If you're in a hurry, you can do all this in a mini food processor.)

▸ Now for the bouillabaisse. Prepare the fish and vegetables before you start. Cut the monkfish into large bite-size pieces and halve the snapper fillets. Wash the clams and mussels in cold water, discarding any that are open. Pull any fibrous beards off the mussels. Set both lots of shellfish aside in a bowl of cold water. Wash the prawns under cold running water.

▸ Chop the onion. Quarter, seed and slice the pepper. Seed and finely chop the chilli. Make a small cross on the underside of each tomato, place in a bowl and cover with boiling water for 30 seconds. Drain, run under cold water to loosen the skins, and peel. Roughly chop the flesh. Peel the potatoes and cut into large dice or 1-cm (½-inch) slices. Soak the saffron in 1 tablespoon hot water.

▸ Heat the olive oil in a large casserole dish, add the onion and cook for 4–5 minutes, until tender but not coloured. Add the pepper, chilli, garlic and spices and continue to cook for a further minute. Add the tomatoes and the saffron infusion and cook gently for 4–5 minutes.

▸ Place the potatoes on top of the vegetables. Arrange the monkfish over the potatoes. Pour in the stock, season and bring to the boil. Cover and simmer for about 10 minutes, until the potatoes are almost tender. Add the mussels, clams, prawns and snapper and continue to cook for a further 5–10 minutes, until all the fish is cooked, the mussels and clams are open, and the prawns have turned a deep pink colour.

▸ Check the seasoning, scatter with the parsley and serve immediately in large, wide warm bowls with the rouille to pass around.

Serves 6
Preparation 20 mins
Cooking 25 mins
275 g (10 oz) monkfish fillets, trimmed
275 g (10 oz) red snapper fillets
500 g (1 lb 2 oz) clams
500 g (1 lb 2 oz) mussels
8–12 raw tiger prawns or king prawns, depending on size
1 onion
1 red pepper
1 large red chilli
4 large ripe tomatoes
650 g (1 lb 6 oz) sweet potatoes and/or waxy small potatoes such as Charlottes
large pinch of saffron threads
4 tablespoons olive oil
2 garlic cloves, crushed
½ teaspoon ground turmeric
½ teaspoon cayenne
1 teaspoon ground cumin
1 teaspoon ground coriander
1.2 litres (2 pints) fish stock
2 tablespoons roughly chopped fresh parsley
salt and freshly ground black pepper

Chilli rouille
pinch of saffron threads
2 large egg yolks
1 teaspoon Dijon mustard
1 garlic clove, crushed
250 ml (8 fl oz) fruity olive oil
1 teaspoon harissa
squeeze of lemon juice, to taste

Good for the good life!
Glorious fish served in true Caribbean style. The colours are vibrant and the aromas are sweet, so let your party swing with this bouillabaisse feast.

Lamb kofta wraps with roasted red pepper hummus

Serves 6
Preparation 25 mins
Cooking 10 mins
50 g (2 oz) fresh breadcrumbs
½ teaspoon dried oregano
50 ml (2 fl oz) dry white wine or
  lemon juice
1 small onion
1 garlic clove, crushed
500 g (1 lb 2 oz) lean minced lamb
3 tablespoons chopped fresh
  flatleaf parsley
½ teaspoon ground cumin
¼ teaspoon cayenne
salt and freshly ground black pepper

Roasted red pepper hummus
1 x 410-g (14-oz) can chick peas,
  drained and rinsed
100 g (4 oz) roasted red pepper
1 garlic clove, crushed
3 tablespoons extra-virgin olive oil
freshly squeezed lemon juice,
  to taste
salt and freshly ground black pepper

To serve
3 ripe tomatoes, chopped
½ red onion, chopped
pinch of cayenne pepper
6 rounded tablespoons Greek
  yoghurt
2 tablespoons chopped fresh mint
6 pitta breads, Mediterranean wraps
  or flat breads
lemon wedges

Good for avoiding a mess
It's hard to make hot spicy
dishes work at a barbeque
or picnic, but wraps are a
great way to eat messy, but
flavoursome ingredients
outdoors.

Kofta are kebabs made with minced meat moulded around a skewer.
When popped inside a wrap they are an exciting addition to alfresco eating as they are perfect 'finger food'.

For convenience, you could buy a jar of roasted red peppers rather than making your own. I like to add a teaspoon of harissa to jazz them up.

▸ Soak 12 wooden skewers in hot water while you prepare the kofta. Place the breadcrumbs in a mixing bowl, add the oregano and white wine or lemon juice and leave to soak for 5 minutes. Roughly chop the onion, tip it into the bowl of a food processor and whiz until finely chopped. Add the garlic, soaked breadcrumbs, lamb, parsley, cumin and cayenne. Season well and whiz again until the mixture is almost smooth and is thoroughly combined.
▸ Tip into a bowl and roll the kofta mixture into 24 walnut-sized balls. Thread two balls on to each wooden skewer, then use your hands to press them firmly into sausage shapes. Cover with cling film and set aside while you make the hummus.
▸ Place the chick peas, roasted peppers garlic and oil in the bowl of a food processor. Season well and whiz until smooth. Add lemon juice to taste and scrape into a bowl.
▸ Preheat the grill. Arrange the kofta on a foil-covered baking tray and grill for about 8 minutes, turning frequently until brown and cooked through. Set aside.
▸ Meanwhile, prepare the accompaniments. Roughly chop the tomatoes and onion, place in a bowl and add the cayenne and some seasoning. In another bowl mix together the yoghurt and mint.
▸ To serve the kofta, split the pitta breads or wraps and fill with a good dollop of hummus and a spoonful of the tomatoes and onions. Add the kofta from two skewers, and some minty yoghurt and serve with a lemon wedge to squeeze over. Accompany with whole pickled chillies and shredded iceberg lettuce.

Puddings, cakes and bakes

Poached peaches with vanilla and sweet Muscat wine

Serves 6
Preparation 10 mins
Cooking 20 mins
100 g (4 oz) caster sugar
2 strips lemon zest
juice of ½ lemon
150 ml (¼ pint) sweet wine,
  such as Muscat
1 vanilla pod
6 ripe peaches

Good for your conscience
A guilt-free, low-fat pudding
that won't sit on the hips.
That means cutting out the
wine, though!

Like plums, peaches belong to the rose family, and during the summer months shops are filled with lots of gorgeous varieties. You don't need to squeeze them to check for ripeness: the sweet smell alone will tell you everything. They also bake and grill beautifully.

I poach my peaches whole, as cutting them beforehand can cause them to break up in the poaching stock, leaving you with a pulpy mess. But by all means cut them in half or into wedges after poaching.

▸ To make the poaching syrup place the sugar, lemon zest and juice and the wine in a deep sauté pan. Split the vanilla pod in half lengthways and add to the pan with 900 ml (1½ pints) water. Bring slowly to the boil to dissolve the sugar, then lower the heat to a very gentle simmer.
▸ Meanwhile, prepare the peaches. Cut a small cross through the skin at the bottom of each one (opposite the stalk end). Place in a large bowl, cover with boiling water and leave for 30–60 seconds to loosen the skin. Rinse under cold water and peel.
▸ Gently lower the peaches into the simmering syrup, cover with a disc of baking parchment and poach for about 15 minutes, until tender (a small sharp knife which should go in relatively easily). The cooking time will vary, depending on the ripeness of the fruit.
▸ Remove the peaches from the pan with a slotted spoon and place in a large bowl. Increase the heat under the poaching syrup and boil until reduced by one-third. Strain over the fruit and leave until cold. Serve the peaches with a swirl of Coulis (page 186).

Shrikhand with poached cardamom apricots

Shrikhand is a form of strained yoghurt from the Gujarat region of India. Use any good-quality natural yoghurt, or Greek yoghurt, which is already strained, if you're in a hurry. Clear honey may be used instead of caster sugar, if preferred.

▸ Set a sieve over a bowl and line it with a couple of layers of clean muslin. Tip the yoghurt into the sieve and cover loosely with cling film. Chill for at least 3 hours, but preferably overnight, by which time the excess liquid will have drained from the yoghurt.

▸ Gently heat the milk in a small pan or in the microwave. Add the saffron and infuse for about 1 hour.

▸ Tip the yoghurt into a mixing bowl, add the saffron milk, 100 g (4 oz) of the sugar and the rosewater. Beat until smooth, taste and add more sugar if you like. Cover and chill until needed.

▸ Place the orange juice and apricots in a saucepan. Add the cardamom pods and remaining sugar. Simmer gently for 5 minutes, then remove from the heat and cool completely.

▸ Divide the *shrikhand* between four bowls, spoon the apricots and orange syrup over it, scatter with the pistachios and serve.

Serves 4
Preparation 5 mins
Cooking 10 mins

2 x 500-g (1 lb 2-oz) pots natural yoghurt
2 tablespoons milk
pinch of saffron
150 g (5 oz) caster sugar, plus extra if needed
1–2 teaspoons rosewater, depending on strength
juice of 3 oranges
300 g (11 oz) ready-to-eat dried apricots
2 cardamom pods, lightly crushed
50 g (2 oz) pistachios, roughly chopped

Fabulous feast: the classics

Why is it that we spend hours and hours preparing a technically difficult pudding, when we often get the best reaction from a simple sponge? Sometimes it's the classics we could cook standing on one leg that are the true crowd pleasers. Times have changed, and we're a lot more experimental with all of our meals these days. But that doesn't mean we don't get nostalgic for the good old basics we used to enjoy as kids. It was important for generations before us to cook for themselves and it shows – we still love their versions of traditional recipes best. Check out my Auntie G's sweet and sour pork (page 115)! Entertaining with a classic theme gives you ample opportunity to personalise the experience so dig out those family recipes and keep your family's food traditions alive.

Menu Ideas

Teatime
French toast, Italian cheese and British bacon sandwich **page 37**
Coconut and lime cupcakes **page 161**

With your Sunday lunch
Bloody Mary prawn and avocado cocktail **page 56**
Mashed potatoes with olive oil and parsley **page 177**
Parsnips with rosemary and honey **page 182**

Early evening meal
Chargrilled steak, asparagus and warm potato salad with salsa verde **page 71**
Teatime pasta with sausage sauce **page 87**
Sweet and sour pork – Auntie G style **page 105**

Desserts
Proper custard **page 189**
Chocolate heaven cake **page 164**
Creamy vanilla rice pudding with stem ginger and rhubarb **page 152**

Creamy vanilla rice pudding with stem ginger and rhubarb

Serves 6
Preparation 5 mins
Cooking 25 mins

1 kilo (2 lb 3 oz) rhubarb
175 g (6 oz) caster sugar
grated zest and juice from 1 orange
150 g (5 oz) pudding rice
1 vanilla pod
600 ml (1 pint) semi-skimmed milk
1 x 142-ml (5-fl oz) pot double cream
1 nugget of stem ginger in syrup,
  finely chopped

My father-in-law's favourite – with a scoop of ice cream and cream, if you please. Lucky it takes so little time to cook.

Pudding rice is a short-grain variety, which absorbs more liquid than the long-grain type, making it ideal for milk puddings.

▸ Preheat the oven to 180°C/350°F/Gas mark 4. Wash the rhubarb in cold water and cut into 4-cm- (1½-in) pieces. Mix with 100g (4oz) of the sugar, the orange zest and juice.
▸ Tip into a ovenproof dish, cover with foil and bake for 25–30 minutes. Remove the foil and cook for a further 5 minutes. Cool to room temperature.
▸ Place the rice in a saucepan, add 350 ml (12 fl oz) water and bring to the boil. Reduce the heat and simmer for 5 minutes. Drain the rice through a sieve and return it to the pan.
▸ Split the vanilla pod in half and add to the rice with the milk and cream. Place over a low heat and bring slowly to the boil. Stir from time to time and simmer very gently for about 20 minutes, until the rice is tender.
▸ Add the rest of the sugar, rhubarb and ginger, and stir to combine.

Quick tip

If, like most connoisseurs, you prefer your pudding to have a crisp, golden skin, pop it under a preheated grill for 3–4 minutes.

Lemon surprise pudding with ginger-spiced cream

Serves 6
Preparation 10 mins
Cooking 45 mins
100 g (4 oz) unsalted butter, softened, plus extra for greasing
150 g (5 oz) caster sugar
grated zest and juice of 3 unwaxed lemons
4 large eggs, separated
75 g (3 oz) self-raising flour
400 ml (14 fl oz) milk

Ginger-spiced cream
600 ml (1 pint) double cream
3 tablespoons syrup from the stem ginger
1 nugget of stem ginger in syrup

This pudding separates during cooking to leave a delicate sponge on top and a lemony custard underneath. If you can't find stem ginger, add a little ginger wine.

▸ In a large bowl cream together the butter and sugar until light and fluffy. Beat in the lemon zest and egg yolks. Sift the flour and fold into the mixture. Add the lemon juice and milk and mix to combine.
▸ Preheat the oven to 180°C/350°F/Gas mark 4.
▸ In a clean bowl whisk the egg whites until they hold stiff peaks. Fold into the lemon mixture using a large metal spoon. Don't worry if the mixture looks slightly curdled. Grease a 1.75-litre (3-pint) dish with butter, tip the lemon mixture into it and bake on the middle shelf of the oven for about 45 minutes, until the top has risen and is, golden and just firm to the touch. Cool for a couple of minutes before serving.
▸ Meanwhile make the ginger-spiced cream. Pour the cream into a large bowl, add the ginger syrup and whip until soft and pillowy using a balloon whisk. Finely dice the stem ginger and fold it into the cream. Spoon into a serving bowl and serve with the lemon surprise pudding.

◗ Super-quick recipe
Frozen strawberry yoghurt

This dessert is lighter and fresher-tasting than ice cream, but its lower fat content means it freezes harder. Allow the dessert to soften in the fridge before serving.

▸ Start by making a light vanilla syrup. Place the sugar and 200 ml (7 fl oz) water in a small saucepan. Split the vanilla pod in half and add to the pan with the orange zest. Slowly bring to the boil, stirring occasionally to dissolve the sugar. Simmer gently for 4–5 minutes, until the syrup has reduced slightly and the various flavours have infused. Remove from the heat and cool.

▸ Hull and roughly chop the strawberries. Tip into a food processor or blender and whiz until smooth. Pour the strawberry purée into a bowl, add the yoghurt and crème fraîche and mix until smooth. Strain the sugar syrup and add to the strawberry mixture according to taste. Remember that it will lose a little sweetness during freezing.

▸ Churn in an ice-cream machine according to the manufacturer's instructions, then transfer to an airtight container and put in the freezer. Alternatively, pour into an airtight container and freeze for a couple of hours. Remove from the freezer and whisk the mixture until it is smooth, breaking up any ice crystals that have formed. Return to the freezer for a further hour, whisk again, then freeze until solid.

▸ Transfer the frozen yoghurt to the fridge to soften for 20 minutes before eating. Serve on its own or with a fresh mixed berry fruit salad.

Serves 6
Preparation 10 mins
Cooking none
100 g (4 oz) caster sugar
½ vanilla pod
2 strips unwaxed orange zest
400 g (14 oz) ripe strawberries
1 x 500-g (1 lb 2-oz) pot natural
    yoghurt
4 tablespoons crème fraîche

Toffee apples

I remember eating my first toffee apple at the local funfair as a child.
It was scrumptious: crackly amber toffee wrapped around a juicy, crisp apple with just enough acidity to make me suck my teeth.

Adult supervision is required if children want to make these, as the toffee reaches extremely high temperatures. A sugar thermometer is really useful, and can be bought quite cheaply at most cook shops. A good tip is to warm the thermometer in hot water before using it as this prevents the glass cracking.

Demerara sugar gives a good toffee taste, but granulated works just as well. For a nutty crunch, dip the toffee-covered apples into toasted nibbed almonds before leaving them to set.

▸ Wash and dry the apples. Twist off the stalks and push a lolly stick or piece of dowelling firmly into the top of each apple.
▸ Place the sugar and 120 ml (4 fl oz) water in a medium saucepan. Set the pan over a low heat to dissolve the sugar, stirring from time to time. Add the vinegar or lemon juice, golden syrup and butter and bring to the boil. Cook without stirring until the syrup reaches the hard crack stage, or 140°C (275°F) on a sugar thermometer. This will take no more than 10 minutes. If you don't have a thermometer, test the syrup by dropping a teaspoonful of it into a cup of cold water: it should harden immediately.
▸ Once the toffee is ready, remove it from the heat and dip one apple at a time into the pan, swirling carefully to coat it completely in the mixture. Allow any excess toffee to drip back into the pan. Set the toffee apples on a parchment-lined baking sheet to harden and cool completely before wrapping in cellophane.

Makes 6–8
Preparation 5 mins
Cooking 15 mins
6 small apples, such as Coxes
   or Braeburns
225 g (8 oz) demerara sugar
1 teaspoon white wine vinegar
   or lemon juice
2 tablespoons golden syrup
25 g (1 oz) unsalted butter

**Good for feeling like
a kid again**
These sugary gems are great for winter parties and will bring out the child in you. Getting the toffee stuck in your teeth is part of the fun.

Chocolate fruit and nut fridge cake

Serves 6–8
Preparation 10 mins
plus cooling time
Cooking 2 mins

350 g (12 oz) plain chocolate
75 g (3 oz) unsalted butter
2 tablespoons clear honey
1 large egg, beaten
250 g (9 oz) mixed dried fruit, such
　　as glacé cherries, ready-to-eat
　　apricots, sultanas and raisins
100 g (4 oz) toasted nuts, such as
　　hazelnuts and almonds
100 g (4 oz) ginger biscuits

As my old pastry chef Aldo would say, 'Respect the *cioccolato*, it's a beautiful thing'. This recipe is very versatile because you can use a mixture of whatever dried fruit and nuts you have to hand. Add a handful of mini marshmallows if you're making the cake for the children, and maybe think about using chocolate with a lower cocoa fat content. I usually add a little extra honey.

Although I've used ginger biscuits here, the recipe would easily work with digestives or oaty biscuits. To make it fancier, add a little chopped stem ginger or finely chopped candied peel.

▸ Line a small roasting tin or 20-cm (8-inch) cake tin with baking parchment or cling film.
▸ Break the chocolate into chunks, place in a heatproof bowl and melt gently, either in a microwave or over a pan of simmering water. (Don't let the bowl touch the water – just let the hot steam melt it.) When nice and smooth, mix in the butter and honey, stirring until melted and thoroughly combined. Slowly beat in the egg for a good minute, then remove from the heat.
▸ Halve the cherries and roughly chop the apricots and nuts. Tip the biscuits into a plastic bag and bash a couple of times with a rolling pin to break them into smallish pieces, not crumbs. Add the nuts, dried fruit and biscuits to the melted chocolate mixture and fold in thoroughly.
▸ Spoon into the prepared tin, level out with a spatula and leave to cool. When cold, cover lightly with cling film and chill until set: normally 3–4 hours. Peel off the cling film and cut into small squares.

Coconut and lime cupcakes

'You put de lime in de coconut and mix it all up' goes the Caribbean song my mum used to sing to me as a kid, and I now sing it with my kids. And their reward for hearing my poor calypso ditty yet again? These lovely iced cupcakes!

For a change, you could swap the lime zest in these cakes for 25 g (1 oz) cocoa powder.

▸ Preheat the oven to 180°C/350°F/Gas mark 4. Line a 12-hole muffin tray with paper cases.
▸ In a large bowl cream together the butter and sugar until pale and light. Gradually add the beaten eggs, mixing well between each addition. Add the lime zest and coconut.
▸ Sift together the flour and baking powder and, using a large metal spoon or rubber spatula, fold these dry ingredients into the creamed mixture and mix until smooth. Divide between the paper cases and bake on the middle shelf of the oven for about 30 minutes, until the cakes are golden and a skewer inserted into the middle of one of them comes out clean. Remove from the oven and cool in the tray for 10 minutes before transferring the cakes to a wire rack until cold.
▸ To make the frosting mix together the mascarpone, icing sugar and lime zest, stirring until smooth. If you are using fresh coconut, peel off the brown skin and grate the flesh on the coarse side of a grater.
▸ Spread an even layer of the mascarpone mixture over the top of each cake and scatter with the fresh coconut or dessicated coconut.

Makes 12
Preparation 15 mins
Cooking 30 mins
175 g (6 oz) unsalted butter, softened
120 g (4½ oz) caster sugar
2 large eggs, beaten
grated zest of 1 unwaxed lime
50 g (2 oz) desiccated coconut
150 g (5 oz) plain flour
1 teaspoon baking powder
2–3 tablespoons milk

Frosting
150 g (5 oz) mascarpone
1 tablespoon icing sugar, sifted
grated zest of 1 unwaxed lime
¼ fresh coconut or 25 g (1 oz)
    desiccated coconut soaked
    in a little milk

Good for getting the kids involved

To save time, you can bake these cakes 24 hours before needed and store them in an airtight box. You can then save the creative icing bit to do with the kids just before serving.

Fresh and fabulous cake therapy

Baking surely has to be the most pleasing and rewarding type of cooking. Just the smell of gingerbread baking in the oven is enough to lift the darkest of moods. How can we resist and why should we? You don't need me to tell you why cake is good, but just in case here are a few inspiring nudges to send you in search of the cake tin!

Make a day of it

Baking is a fantastic feel-good activity. Get the kids involved by making something fun and messy. Choose simple recipes so you can spend the time being creative with the icing! I also recommend taking time out for yourself with some peaceful comfort baking for one.

Bake, don't buy

Instead of reaching into your purse and pockets for the vending machine, make a batch of cookies once a week and you should have enough to pop one or two in your lunch box every day.

A cake a day keeps the doctor away

By making your own cakes and bakes you can be sure of exactly what goes into them. Sometimes it takes ten bad biscuits to cure a craving, when one good one could do the trick. Kiss goodbye to artificial hidden nasties, and say hello to your special customized treat loaded with nuts, oats and other goodies.

Cake karma

Cakes and bakes are made for sharing, although I'm sure that there are plenty of us who'd attempt to eat a whole tray of brownies on their own given the choice. Home-baked goodies make perfect gifts too – wrap some cookies or cupcakes in a pretty box, tie with a bright ribbon and wait for the smiles!

Cake fixes

If a cake isn't broken, don't try to fix it. Classic baked goods have been tried-and-tested by generations of cake-lovers. They can really hit the spot, be it at a celebration, a dinner party, cheering up a friend in need, or adding a bit of sunshine to a dreary day. Flapjacks and oat-based cakes are good for energy fixes, cupcakes are great for quick fixes and chocolate is good for fixing just about anything!

Chocolate heaven cake

Serves 8+
Preparation 20 mins
Cooking 25 mins
100 g (4 oz) dark chocolate
150 g (5 oz) unsalted butter,
    softened, plus extra for greasing
175 g (6 oz) golden caster sugar
3 large eggs, beaten
1 teaspoon vanilla extract
225 g (8 oz) plain flour
1 teaspoon baking powder
½ teaspoon bicarbonate of soda
2 tablespoons cocoa powder
200 ml (7 fl oz) sour cream,
    at room temperature

Frosting
350 g (12 oz) dark chocolate
225 g (8 oz) unsalted butter, softened
500 g (1 lb 2 oz) icing sugar, sifted
1 teaspoon vanilla extract
225 ml (8 fl oz) milk

**Good for the ultimate
feel-good experience**
If you are going to treat
yourself, do it properly.
Sometimes feeling good
is about pure indulgence
and chocolate is sure to
hit the spot.

All that stuff about a moment on the lips, a lifetime on the hips rings true here, but hey! – it's not an everyday indulgence. This heavenly cake is great for a birthday or teatime treat, but you could also serve it as a pudding.

All cake-baking requires a little advance thought, so make sure the butter is soft and the eggs and sour cream are at room temperature before starting to mix. If you have only two cake tins, it doesn't matter – just divide the mixture between them and bake for a little longer: the skewer test will tell you when they're done. You can make this cake the day before it's needed and do the frosting when you're about to serve it.

▸ Preheat the oven to 180°C/350°F/Gas mark 4. Grease 3 x 20-cm (8-inch) sandwich tins with butter and line the bases with greased baking parchment.
▸ Break the chocolate into chunks and melt in a heatproof bowl, either on a low setting in the microwave or over a pan of barely simmering water. Remove from the heat, stir until smooth and cool slightly.
▸ In a large bowl cream together the butter and sugar until pale and fluffy (this is easiest using a hand-held electric mixer). Gradually add the eggs, mixing well after each addition. Add the vanilla extract and melted chocolate and mix until smooth.
▸ Sieve together the flour, baking powder, bicarbonate of soda and cocoa. Using a large metal spoon, fold the dry ingredients into the creamed mixture in alternate batches with the sour cream. Mix well between each addition, scraping down the bowl with a rubber spatula.
▸ Divide the mixture evenly between the prepared tins, level with a palette knife and bake for about 25 minutes, until the cakes are springy to the touch and a skewer inserted into the middle of one of them comes out clean. Cool for 5 minutes in the tins, then turn out on to a wire rack to cool completely.
▸ Once the cakes are completely cold, make the frosting. In a large bowl mix the butter with the chocolate chunks. Set the bowl over a pan of barely simmering water, not allowing the bottom of the bowl to touch the water. Melt until smooth, stirring occasionally. In another bowl, whisk together the icing sugar, vanilla extract and milk until completely smooth. Add the melted chocolate and butter and mix until combined. Set aside for about 30 minutes to thicken slightly.
▸ Place one of the cakes on a serving plate and spread with a little frosting. Cover with another cake and more frosting. Top with the remaining cake and lightly press all the cake layers together. Use a palette knife to spread the remaining frosting evenly over the top and sides of the cake.

Fizzy fruit jellies with blackcurrant ripple cream

When I was a child I just loved wobbly jelly and cream. I've fizzed it up for my kids by making it with sparkling water. For adults replace this with champagne or sparkling wine. If you're in a hurry, you can use a 135-g (4¾-oz) packet of jelly, replacing 600 ml (1 pint) of the boiling water with fizzy water.

▸ Place the blackcurrants in a sauté pan and add 200 ml (7 fl oz) tap water and the sugar. Set over a low heat and cook very gently for about 10 minutes, until the currants have burst. Remove from the heat and tip the contents of the pan into a fine sieve set over a bowl. Leave the fruit to drain for 10 minutes to ensure that all the juice collects in the bowl. Do not help it along by stirring.

▸ Pour the juice into a measuring jug and add enough sparkling water to make the liquid up to 900 ml (1½ pints). Press the blackcurrants through the sieve, taste for sweetness, adding a little sugar if needed, and set aside.

▸ Place the gelatine in a shallow dish, cover with cold water and leave to soak for 5 minutes, or until soft.

▸ Pour one-third of the blackcurrant juice into a saucepan and warm over a medium heat. Squeeze any excess water from the gelatine, then whisk the gelatine into the pan until completely dissolved. Pour the gelatine mixture into the remaining blackcurrant juice and mix until thoroughly combined. Cool until just starting to set, then whisk the jelly mixture incorporating the small air bubbles. Divide between six glasses, cover loosely with cling film and chill for at least 2 hours, or until set.

▸ Meanwhile, lightly whip the cream in a large bowl. Add the reserved blackcurrant purée and lightly fold it in so that the cream is rippled with colour. Spoon into a bowl and serve with the fizzy fruit jellies.

Serves 6
Preparation 30 mins
Cooking 10 mins
500 g (1 lb 2 oz) blackcurrants
100 g (4 oz) caster sugar, plus extra if needed
1 bottle sparkling elderflower water or sparkling wine
5 sheets leaf gelatine
600 ml (1 pint) double cream

Brownies

These brownies are dense, very chocolatey and packed full of fruit and nuts. If dried cherries are hard to find, use raisins instead.

Makes 16–20
Preparation 15 mins
Cooking 25–30 mins
150 g (5 oz) walnut pieces
175 g (6 oz) unsalted butter,
    plus extra for greasing
200 g (7 oz) dark chocolate
200g (7 oz) caster sugar
3 large eggs
1 teaspoon vanilla extract
150 g (5 oz) plain flour
1 teaspoon baking powder
100 g (4 oz) plain chocolate chips
150 g (5 oz) dried cherries

Good for a midnight feast
Eat brownies American-style:
as a late-night treat with a
dollop of ice cream and a
glass of cold milk. Delicious.

▸ Preheat the oven to 180°C/350°F/Gas mark 4. Grease a 30 x 23 x 4-cm (12 x 9 x 1½ inch) baking tin with butter and line the base and sides with baking parchment.
▸ Toast the walnuts in the oven for 5 minutes (set the timer because it's easy to forget them). Remove from the oven and cool.
▸ Melt the butter and chocolate together, either on medium power in the microwave or in a heatproof bowl set over a pan of barely simmering water. Stir until smooth and cool.
▸ In a large bowl beat together the sugar, eggs and vanilla extract until pale and thick. Add the cooled chocolate mixture and stir until smooth.
▸ Sift the plain flour and baking powder into the chocolate mixture and fold in, using a large metal spoon. Add the walnuts, chocolate chips and cherries and mix until thoroughly combined.
▸ Pour into the prepared tin and spread level. Bake on the middle shelf of the oven for about 25–30 minutes. Cool in the tin before cutting into squares.

Prunes and figs infused in tea with vanilla pod yoghurt

Prunes are great for soaking up flavours and develop a lovely plumpness in the process. Even dried figs recapture some of their bloom and lusciousness after being soaked.

It's hard to believe that prunes used to be more popular than plums, but that was the case a few hundred years ago. Although the idea of prunes and figs infused with tea might sound a little strange, the flavour is quite subtle and you'll be hooked once you try it. The best prunes come from Agen in France, but Californian ones are great too. For a change, soft dried apricots are also good in this recipe.

Serves 4–6
Preparation 10 mins + cooling time
Cooking 10 mins
2 Earl Grey tea bags
4 tablespoons brandy, port or
    Marsala
100 g (4 oz) caster sugar
2 strips unwaxed lemon zest
1 small cinnamon stick
1 small sprig fresh rosemary
250 g (9 oz) soft Agen prunes
150 g (5 oz) soft dried figs
1 x 200-g (7-oz) pot Greek yoghurt
1 vanilla pod

▸ Bring 600 ml (1 pint) water to the boil in a medium-sized saucepan. Remove from the heat, add the tea bags and steep for 10 minutes.
▸ Remove the tea bags from the pan and add the brandy, port or Marsala, and the sugar, lemon zest, cinnamon and rosemary to the tea. Tip in the prunes and figs, bring to the boil, then reduce the heat and simmer very gently for 5 minutes.
▸ Meanwhile, put the yoghurt in a bowl, then split the vanilla pod lengthways and scrape the tiny black seeds into the yoghurt pot. Mix well.
▸ Remove the pan from the heat and set aside until the tea is completely cold and the fruit has plumped up. Remove the lemon zest, cinnamon and rosemary. Serve in glass dishes with the vanilla pod yoghurt or fromage frais.

Side orders

Stir-fried broccoli with garlic, ginger and spices

Serves 4
Preparation 2 mins
Cooking 5 mins
300 g (10 oz) tenderstem broccoli,
    trimmed
2 tablespoons olive oil
1 teaspoon crushed dried chilli
1 teaspoon cumin seeds
½ teaspoon mustard seeds
1 clove garlic, crushed
1 teaspoon grated fresh ginger
salt and freshly ground black pepper

Broccoli has a lovely texture and combined with the sharp ginger and garlic, this dish is sure to get your stir fries sizzling.

▸ Bring a large pan of salted water to the boil. Add the broccoli and cook for 1–2 minutes until just tender then drain well in a colander.
▸ Heat the oil in a wok or large sauté pan. Add the chilli, cumin seeds and mustard seeds and cook over a medium heat for 30 seconds until the spices are fragrant. Add the garlic and ginger and cook for a further 30 seconds. Add the drained broccoli and stir-fry for 1 minute until tender and well coated in the spices. Serve immediately.

Roasted Ramiro peppers stuffed with goats' cheese and garlic crumbs

You say Romano, I say Ramiro . . . and before you burst into song you should know that these two names are actually describing the same thing: some supermarkets just like to be different. The sweetness of these peppers is enhanced by roasting, and a little bit of pesto spread inside the pepper halves before they are stuffed is a lovely addition.

▸ Preheat the oven to 200°C/400°F/Gas mark 6.
▸ Cut each pepper in half through the stalk and lay cut-side uppermost on a baking tray. Season and drizzle with a little of the oil. Cook on the middle shelf of the oven for about 10–15 minutes, until tender.
▸ Meanwhile, mix together the parsley, basil, garlic, capers and breadcrumbs. Add the remaining oil and season well.
▸ Divide the breadcrumb mixture evenly between each pepper half. Crumble over the goat's cheese and return to the oven for about 15 minutes, until the breadcrumbs and cheese are golden brown.

Serves 4
Preparation 10 mins
Cooking 30 mins
2 Ramiro peppers
3 tablespoons extra-virgin olive oil
2 tablespoons chopped fresh flatleaf parsley
1 tablespoon chopped fresh basil
1 fat garlic clove, crushed
2 teaspoons capers, rinsed and roughly chopped
50 g (2 oz) fresh breadcrumbs
50–75 g (2–3 oz) crumbly goats' cheese
salt and freshly ground black pepper

Creamed flageolet beans

Serves 6
Preparation 5 mins
Cooking 10 mins
3 x 410-g (14½ -oz) flageolet beans
1 tablepoon olive oil
2 large shallots, finely chopped
1 fat garlic clove, crushed
100 ml (3½ fl oz) vegetable
   chicken stock
3 tablespoons chopped
   flatleaf parsley
salt and freshly ground pepper

Although canned beans are suggested for convenience, you can use dried beans if you prefer. Just soak them overnight in plenty of cold water and cook them according to the packet instructions.

▸ Drain the flageolet beans in a colander and rinse well under cold running water. Set aside.
▸ Heat the olive oil, add the shallots and cook over a medium heat for about 2–3 minutes until tender, but not coloured. Add the garlic and continue to cook for another 30 seconds.
▸ Add the stock and rinsed beans, bring to the boil, reduce the heat to a simmer and cook for about 5 minutes, until tender. Tip the contents of the pan into a food processor and whiz until smooth. Season well and stir in the parsley. Serve immediately.

● Super-quick recipe
Garlicky cannellini beans

Serves 4–6
Preparation 5 mins
Cooking 10 mins
2 tablespoons olive oil
2 shallots, finely chopped
1 garlic clove, crushed
2 x 400-g (14-oz) can cannellini
   beans, drained and rinsed
100 ml (3½ fl oz) chicken or
   vegetable stock
2 tablespoons chopped fresh parsley
squeeze of lemon juice
salt and freshly ground black pepper

These luscious beans are a great source of protein. Just remember your mints for afterwards.

▸ Heat the oil in a saucepan, add the shallots and garlic and cook for 2–3 minutes, until tender but not coloured.
▸ Add the cannellini beans and stock, bring to the boil, then simmer for about 4 minutes, until the beans are tender and heated through. Add the parsley and lemon juice, season and serve immediately.

Mashed potatoes with olive oil and parsley

There's no doubt that mashed potato is one of the best-ever comfort foods – but consistency is everything. I like mine without lumps, which is easily achieved with an electric mixer. The garlic in this mash lightly infuses the oil, so it is not overpowering, but you could leave it out if it's not your thing. For an extra-creamy finish, add a few tablespoons of double cream.

▸ Place the potatoes in a large saucepan, cover with cold water, add a large pinch of salt and bring to the boil. Half-cover the pan and cook over a medium heat for about 25 minutes, until the potatoes are tender when tested with the point of a knife.
▸ Meanwhile, pour the oil into a small pan and add the garlic. Heat gently over a low heat for 5 minutes to allow the garlic to infuse the oil. Remove from the heat and cool slightly.
▸ Drain the potatoes through a colander, return to the pan and cover with a clean tea towel. Set aside for about 3 minutes to allow the potatoes to steam dry.
▸ Mash the potatoes until smooth, using a potato ricer or, for the creamiest mash ever, a hand-held electric mixer. Add the milk and parsley and season well. Strain the oil into the potatoes and beat until smooth. Serve immediately.

Serves 6
Preparation 5 mins
Cooking 35 mins
1.5 kg (3¼ lb) floury potatoes, peeled and quartered
8 tablespoons fruity olive oil
2 garlic cloves, sliced
150 ml (¼ pint) milk
3 tablespoons chopped fresh parsley
salt and freshly ground white pepper

● Super-quick recipe
Pak choi with honey, soy and sesame seeds

Originally from China, pak choi is a member of the cabbage family, yet has a wonderful mild, nutty and uncabbage-like flavour when cooked. It's great for stir-fries or steaming.

To save time, you can buy sesame seeds already toasted. Fresh ginger keeps really well in the freezer: just take it out, grate what you need while it's still frozen, then pop it back into the freezer. Try not to leave it out or it will turn into a soggy sponge.

▸ Toast the sesame seeds in a dry frying pan over a medium heat, stirring with a wooden spoon, for about 2 minutes, until golden. Remove from the heat, tip on to a plate and set aside.
▸ If necessary, lightly trim the pak choi and rinse under cold running water. Cut lengthways into four or six pieces, keeping the root intact.
▸ Heat the oil in a wok or large sauté pan. Add the ginger and garlic and cook for 30 seconds. Add the pak choi and stir-fry quickly for 1–2 minutes, until the leaves are tender. Add the honey and soy sauce and continue to cook for a further 30 seconds. Tip on to a serving dish, scatter with the toasted sesame seeds and serve immediately.

Serves 4
Preparation 3 mins
Cooking 5 mins
1 tablespoon sesame seeds
4 heads pak choi
2 teaspoons sesame oil
1 teaspoon grated fresh ginger
1 garlic clove, crushed
1 tablespoon clear honey
2 tablespoons soy sauce

Lemon and tahini dressing

Serves 4–6
Preparation 10 mins
Cooking none
4 tablespoons extra-virgin olive oil
3 tablespoons Greek yoghurt
2 tablespoons tahini paste
juice of ½ lemon
1 clove garlic, crushed
½ teaspoon gound cumin
pinch of cayenne
salt and freshly ground black pepper

Tahini – or, if you like, tahina – is a thick, beige oily ground sesame seed paste that is very similar to a smooth peanut butter texture and is the basis to hummus. It also goes well with a blend of parsley, garlic and lemon juice to make a great dip.

▸ Combine all of the ingredients in a bowl and whisk until smooth. Taste and season with salt and freshly ground black pepper.

Hollandaise sauce

Serves 6
Preparation 2 mins
Cooking 10 mins
225 g (8 oz) unsalted butter
3 tablespoons white wine vinegar
3 large egg yolks
juice of ½ lemon
salt and ground white pepper

While working in French kitchens I learnt that hollandaise sauce is the base from which many other sauces derive. Add some tarragon, chervil and lemon juice for sauce béarnaise; to that add some fine diced tomatoes for sauce choron; or add a dollop of English mustard for a sauce that is fabulous with boiled gammon. The permutations go on and on.

Of course, straight Hollandaise is divine with poached salmon, steamed vegetables (especially asparagus), or as a dip for chunky hot chips!

▸ Gently melt the butter over a low heat, then remove and cool slightly.
▸ Place the vinegar and 2 tablespoons water in a small pan and reduce by half over a low to medium heat. Pour into a medium-sized heatproof bowl, add the egg yolks and whisk until combined. Set the bowl over a pan of barely simmering water without allowing it actually to touch the water. Using a balloon whisk, beat the mixture until pale, thick and foamy.
▸ Add the melted butter, no more than 1 tablespoon at a time, whisking constantly between each addition. When all the butter has been incorporated the sauce should be thick and creamy. Whisk in the lemon juice and season to taste.

Fabulous side orders: breaking the rules

How many times have we heard or been told that we should only have white wine with fish or rich red burgundy with meat? At last we've discovered the rules can be broken and the same applies to side orders. Long gone are the days when you'd go to a restaurant and everyone would get the same side dishes of two veg, no matter what their main course was. Nowadays, there's so much more to think about when it comes to side orders and it can be one of the most exciting aspects of cooking. It's such a shame to make so much effort on a fantastic roast fillet of beef, for example, only to serve it with plain old potatoes and boiled peas. Mix and match whatever side orders take your fancy.

Potato-tastic
Just think how potatotes can transform an ordinary dish into something mouth-watering – mash, especially, can be jazzed up to suit your potato passions. It's only when all the textures and flavours of food ooze together that a dish become truly feel-good so don't deny yourself this essential comfort food.

Fruity
Don't forget that fresh fruit has just as much texture and flavour as vegetables. When combining your side orders remember how fruit can instantly add a bitter, sweet or sharp taste – check out my substantial **Roquefort, apple and walnut salad** (page 66).

Be adventurous
Try introducing veggies that you (or the kids) might not have considered. Never tried celeriac before? Give it a whirl in my **Celeriac remoulade with prawns and French beans** (page 40). Think and experiment – you'll be surprised at what you achieve and, ultimately, enjoy cooking all the more.

Get saucy
Sauces add a new dimension to your food. Don't drown out the flavour of the dish by going over the top with a gooey covering of sauce, but instead try impressing your guests by choosing something simple, but different from the traditional option. A unique twist on a classic sauce can really turn a dish into something magical.

Parsnips roasted with rosemary and honey

Serves 4
Preparation 5 mins
Cooking 45 mins
40 g (1½ oz) butter
1 tablespoon olive oil
4 medium parsnips, peeled
 and quartered
1 tablespoon clear honey
3 teaspoons chopped fresh
 rosemary leaves
salt and freshly ground black pepper

Available from early autumn until spring, parsnips are at their best in the middle of winter, when their ivory skin has been touched by frost. Avoid buying any that are dry-looking or have brown patches.

The honey brings out the natural sweetness of the parsnips, which are perfect with roast chicken or lamb.

▸ Preheat the oven to 200°C/400°F/Gas mark 6.
▸ Heat the butter and oil in a medium-sized roasting tin on the middle shelf of the oven. Add the parsnips and seasoning, then turn to coat in the hot fat. Cook for about 40 minutes, until golden brown, turning the parsnips halfway through the cooking time.
▸ Remove the roasting tin from the oven, add the honey and rosemary to the roasting tin and mix so that the parsnips are well coated. Return the tin to the oven and cook for a further 5 minutes. Serve immediately.

Blue cheese sables

Makes about 40
Preparation 10 mins
Cooking 25 mins
175 g (6 oz) plain flour
25 g (1 oz) polenta
½ teaspoon English mustard powder
½ teaspoon cayenne
150g (5 oz) cold butter, diced
1 tablespoon poppy seeds (optional)
100 g (4 oz) blue cheese, crumbled
50 g (2 oz) freshly grated Parmesan
salt and freshly ground black pepper

These gorgeous, sandy-textured biscuits are perfect as a pre-dinner nibble with a martini or glass of chilled white wine. Try topping them with a slice of cherry tomato and a small dollop of pesto or tapenade.

I like to use a crumbly rather than creamy blue cheese. Stilton works well and has never let me down, but you can use Cheddar if you find Stilton too strong. Once made, sables will keep in an airtight container for several days.

▸ Tip the flour, polenta, mustard, cayenne and butter into the bowl of a food processor and add seasoning. Using the pulse button, process until the mixture resembles fine breadcrumbs.
▸ Add the poppy seeds (if using), three-quarters of the blue cheese and half of the Parmesan. Add 1 tablespoon cold water and pulse again until the dough comes together. Tip out on to a clean work surface and knead very lightly to shape the dough into a ball. Divide into two equal portions and roll each into a large sausage shape no thicker than 5 cm (2 inches). Cover with cling film and chill for 1–2 hours, until fairly solid, or pop into the freezer until needed.
▸ Preheat the oven to 180°C/350°F/Gas mark 4 and line two baking sheets with baking parchment.
▸ Slice each sausage of dough into about 1-cm (½-inch) slices and place on the baking sheets, leaving at least 2.5 cm (1 inch) between each slice. Scatter a little of the remaining blue cheese in the centre of each sable and bake on the middle shelf of the oven for about 20 minutes, or until the edges are golden brown and the cheese is bubbling gently. Cool the sables on the baking sheets, then transfer to an airtight container until needed.

● Super-quick recipe
Home-made pesto

Nothing quite matches the quality of home-made. With home-made pesto you get a greener colour and more vibrant flavour, especially during summer when basil is in season and perhaps even growing in the garden. If the pesto is not needed immediately, it can be covered and will keep for a week in the fridge.

▸ Place the basil, garlic and pine nuts in the bowl of a food processor and whiz until roughly chopped. With the machine still running, add the olive oil in a steady stream.
▸ Add the Parmesan and whiz again until smooth. Taste and season: you may not need to add much salt if the Parmesan is very salty.

Serves 4
Preparation 5 mins
Cooking none
50 g (2 oz) fresh basil
1 garlic clove, crushed
25 g (1 oz) pine nuts
120 ml (4 fl oz) fruity olive oil
6 tablespoons freshly grated
  Parmesan
salt and freshly ground black pepper

● Super-quick recipe
Shallot vinaigrette

So simple, and yet so useful. This dressing can be used to flavour any type of salad. Try to source a good-quality extra-virgin olive oil – it's well worth the extra cost.

▸ Place all the ingredients in a screw-top jar and shake vigorously for 15–20 seconds. The vinaigrette is now ready to use, or can be stored in the fridge until needed.

Makes 300 ml (½ pint) approx.
Preparation 1 min
Cooking none
3 teaspoons Dijon mustard
2 teaspoons soft light brown sugar
85 ml (3 fl oz) white wine vinegar
  or tarragon vinegar
1–2 shallots, finely chopped
200 ml (7 fl oz) extra-virgin olive oil
salt and freshly ground black pepper

Raspberry and redcurrant coulis

Serves 4–6
Preparation 2 mins
Cooking 2 mins
150 g (5 oz) redcurrants
1–2 tablespoons caster sugar
150 g (5 oz) raspberries

What can be more glorious than seeing the first raspberries of the season? In Britain, the first rasperries tend to appear around May and are a nice reminder that summer is around the corner.

▸ Remove the redcurrants from their stalks and place in a small saucepan. Add 1 tablespoon of the sugar and cook over a low heat until the redcurrants are tender and juicy. Tip into a blender, add the raspberries and whiz until smooth.
▸ Pour the coulis into a nylon sieve, then use the back of a spoon to push it into a bowl. Taste and add a little more sugar if needed.

Proper custard

Officially known as *crème anglaise*, **proper custard** isn't a bit like the stuff that comes out of packets. It has a wonderfully rich flavour, and can accompany any number of cold and hot desserts. It also makes a great base for vanilla ice cream, and can be flavoured in various ways (by adding melted bitter chocolate, for example). Once made, cooled, sprinkled with a little caster sugar (to prevent a skin forming) and covered in cling film, this custard will keep in the fridge for up to 48 hours.

▸ Pour the milk into a saucepan. Split the vanilla pod in half and add to the pan. Bring slowly to the boil, then remove from the heat and leave to one side for 20 minutes.

▸ Beat the egg yolks and sugar in a large bowl until pale and creamy with a ribbon consistency. Pour the milk on to the egg mixture, whisking constantly until smooth. Pour the mixture back into the saucepan, place over a low heat and cook gently, stirring constantly with a wooden spoon until the custard is thick enough to coat the back of the spoon and your finger leaves a trail when you run it down the spoon.

▸ Remove the vanilla pod, strain the custard into a jug to remove any stringy eggy bits and serve immediately.

Serves 4–6
Preparation 5 mins + 20 mins infusing
Cooking 10 mins
600 ml (1 pint) full-cream milk
1 vanilla pod
5 large egg yolks
50 g (2 oz) caster sugar

Index

Page references in **bold** denote photographs.

Acknowledgements

It's so important to acknowledge all those involved in this book because without them it would not have been possible.

To my lovely food stylist Annie Rigg who ended up shopping and cooking with me at all times of the day and night. Boy, did we have some great nibbles!

To my food photographer Francesca Yorke for her delicious and spontaneous photographs that really bring the food alive – so much so you could almost eat the pages.

To Alex, Allan, Emma, Jim, Katrin and Saskia at Smith & Gilmour.

To all of those at BBC Books for believing in my new project: from the outset my commissioning editor Nicky Ross, and then Stuart Cooper, some bird called Eleanor Maxfield, and many others who have greatly contributed.

To my friends, the stallholders at Borough Market, for selling and producing food the way it should be.

To my agent and friends at JHA: Jerry 'Eggs Benedict' Hicks, Sarah, Julie, Charlotte and Emma – who are as close to me as my family.

And, of course, to my wonderful wife Clare and my kids, who inspire me in more ways than I could have ever imagined. (Sorry about the late nights in the study, the messy kitchen and seriously overloaded fridges!) And finally, to my dog Oscar, who's getting a little old and a touch fat – we both don't run as quickly as we used to!